Telling Our Story

The Arab American National Museum

Telling Our Story

The Arab American National Museum

All inquiries should be addressed to:
The Arab American National Museum
13624 Michigan Avenue
Dearborn, Michigan 48126
www.arabamericanmuseum.org

Printed and bound in Canada

ISBN 978-0-9767977-1-5

10 9 8 7 6 5 4 3 2 1

The AANM documents, preserves, celebrates and educates the public on the history, life, culture, and contributions of Arab Americans. We serve as a resource to enhance the knowledge and understanding about Arab Americans and their presence in the United States.

Acknowledgements

Establishing the Arab American National Museum was a long and challenging process. This monumental project could not have succeeded without the support of hundreds of people including museum experts, scholars, community members and staff. While I would be remiss if I did not acknowledge everyone who went out of his/her way to support us, it is almost impossible to mention them all.

As soon as we started the planning process for establishing the Museum, we approached Steve Hamp, who was at the time the president and CEO of the Henry Ford Museum and Greenfield Village (recently renamed The Henry Ford) and Irene Hirano, the president and CEO of the Japanese American National Museum. Both made themselves and their senior staff available to us throughout the planning years and even after we opened. We will forever be indebted to them and to their staff.

There were also a number of scholars who patiently pointed us to the accurate resources, reviewed the exhibits' text, and provided us with missing information. These included Dr. Jack Shaheen, Dr. May Seikaly, Dr. Janice Terry and Dr. Yvonne Lockwood. Additionally, special consultant and historian Dr. Michael Suleiman provided us with unpublished information that enriched our exhibits and curator Elsie Peck helped us in the "Contributions of the Arab World" exhibit.

During the planning process we also established the Museum Task Force, a local advisory board of members of the Arab American community, scholars and museum experts, who met regularly for almost four years and provided us with valuable advice and important contacts throughout the country. They were extremely instrumental in guiding the planning, research and fundraising efforts.

Of course the Museum could not have been built without the hard work and dedication of the Museum staff including curator Sarah Blannett, who kept the project moving, grant writer Greta Anderson who kept the funding coming, researcher Sarah Rogers and other staff members including Deana Rabia, Suzy Mazloum and Celine Taminian to mention only a few.

For this publication, Alma Khasawnih was extremely helpful in reviewing the text, selecting and organizing all the photos and images included in this publication. Her efforts were critical in bringing this publication to fruition. Special thanks to Fay Saad for her help in proofreading and other logistics. Many of the beautiful pictures of exhibits and artifacts included in this publication were taken by photographer Bill Mcdad and Devon Akmon.

This publication and the Arab American National Museum are supported, in part, by *Artography: Arts in a Changing America*, a grant and documentation program of Leveraging Investments in Creativity, funded by the Ford Foundation. This publication is also supported, in part, by the Ford Fund.

On a personal level, I am grateful to my husband and friend Noel Saleh, not only for his support during these very demanding years, but also for his help in reading text, reviewing grants, making phone calls and doing whatever he could to help; ACCESS leadership, who trusted me to successfully bring this project to fruition; and my two colleagues and partners on this project, Ismael Ahmed and Maha Freij. I am most grateful to the hundreds of people who helped us make this dream a reality by giving generously of their time, money and family treasures. Together, we were able share a vision and create a Museum that our community can be proud of: an educational and cultural institution that welcomes as it informs; entertains as it educates; a place where Arab and non-Arab can learn more about Arab Americans, their history, culture, and their great contributions to our nation.

Anan Ameri
Founding Director

Foreword

Ismael Ahmed
CEO, ACCESS

For over 35 years, the Arab Community Center for Economic and Social Services (ACCESS) has defined itself as an organization that builds human capacity. From the beginning, we believed that arts and culture were integral to that building process.

Early on, we were involved in cross-cultural activities with other communities. In 1987, we launched a cultural arts program that grew into a full-fledged cultural arts department. We began to produce regular programs and events including the annual Dearborn Arab International Festival and the Concert of Colors—a free, three-day music festival featuring performers from around the world.

Over the last several years, we focused on mainstreaming Arab culture and building relationships with other communities, with an emphasis on promoting the understanding of Arab Americans and the Arab World.

By early 2000, ACCESS had become one of the largest service providers in metro Detroit, recognized for its work in social services, mental health, education, employment, legal, and medical services, as well as the arts. In many ways, ACCESS became a player on the national stage, establishing itself as one of the go-to organizations in terms of Arab American arts.

As we began to plan for the future, we asked ourselves what areas of work would make the greatest impact and change the paradigm for Arab Americans.

We started by developing the National Network of Arab American Communities working with a group of Arab American community organizations across the country that offer human services, advocacy and arts programming. The next step was to build an institution that would serve as the leading source for enhancing knowledge and understanding of Arab Americans and the Arab world—*an institution that would tell our story.*

There were many thoughts and ideas on how to proceed. We thought it was important to communicate and institutionalize the story of Arab Americans—*what they contributed, where they came from and their potential as Arab Americans.* It was pivotal that we tell our own story in a way that reflected the tremendous contributions that Arab Americans have made in this country.

ACCESS leaders concluded that the best way to institutionalize the Arab American experience was to create the Arab American National Museum. This led to the task of fundraising and consensus building around the country.

We brought people together from around the United States, something that had not been done until now. Many said the community was too diverse to cooperate or that we could not raise the $16.8 million needed to build a museum. Still others said we would never agree on a single story. Today, the Museum stands as a shining example that Arab Americans can collaborate to launch these important institutions that are so necessary for our survival in America.

The future of the Arab American National Museum and the Arab American community itself is dependent on learning the lessons from this project. If we act together to raise the necessary resources and human capital, we can in fact change the entrenched paradigm of stereotyping and powerlessness that seriously and negatively affects the quality of life for Arab Americans on a daily basis.

Telling Our Story:
The Arab American National Museum

Anan Ameri

Director, AANM

When I uncovered the stories of my family, particularly the women's stories, I knew my life's work was presenting itself to me. Not only in the particular, but as these narratives represent many of our stories, of women who are left behind, and must find their own way. My mother and grandmother had a kind of bravery I couldn't possibly imagine; yet, I see new immigrants going through the same struggle and it connects me to a larger community.
— Elmaz Abinader

On May 5, 2005, the Arab American community celebrated the inauguration of the first-ever Arab American National Museum (AANM). The museum, which was in the making for more than five years, is located in the heart of the Arab American community in Dearborn[1], Michigan, across the street from the Dearborn City Hall, a rather symbolic location in a city that had been historically hostile to ethnic and racial minorities, including Arab Americans.

While this introduction is about the story of creating the Arab American National Museum, this publication is about the three thematic permanent exhibits of the Museum. It brings to our readers the untold stories of Arab Americans who have been an integral part of the American society since its inception. These are the stories of courageous men and women who came to the United States seeking better lives for themselves and their families; they are also the stories of these immigrants' children and grandchildren.

Building the Arab American National Museum and bringing to life these amazingly powerful stories was not a simple undertaking. While ACCESS[2] is the largest Arab American organization in the United States, and it enjoys strong local and national support, it is, after all, primarily a social service organization. And while ACCESS had a well-established Cultural Arts Department since 1987, we were aware that building and running a museum would be a much more challenging endeavor. None of us involved in the vision and planning came from a museum background. However, we knew that Arab Americans and their contributions have been excluded from our history books, and we were determined to include them. We wanted to give our people the recognition they well deserve. We recognized that what we lacked in museum experience, we would make up for by having the vision, passion, conviction, work ethic, and determination.

Why an Arab American Museum?

The last few decades had witnessed the creation of a number of ethnic museums including the Charles H. Wright Museum of African American History in Detroit, the Wing Luke Museum in Seattle, the Japanese American National Museum in Los Angeles and the Smithsonian Institution's National Museum of the American Indian in Washington, D.C., to mention only a few. These culturally specific institutions are for the most part a response to the exclusion of minorities from mainstream institutions, including museums.

The Arab American population is estimated at 4.2 million, 490,000 of whom live in Michigan. It is clear that Arab Americans represent a significant group within our population. In spite of the fact that there are an estimated 17,000 museums in the United States, there was not a single museum that documented the history and contributions of Arab Americans. Recognizing the importance of museums in educating the public, we felt the need to establish the Arab American National Museum as an educational and cultural institution that tells the stories of Arab Americans.

By bringing the voices and faces of Arab Americans to mainstream audiences, the AANM is committed to dispelling many of the misconceptions about Arab Americans and other minorities. The Museum brings to light the shared experiences of immigrants and ethnic groups, thus paying tribute to the diversity of our nation. It also addresses the need to provide the public with accurate information about Arabs and Arab Americans, which is not often widely disseminated.

Planning for the Museum

Once a decision was made to establish the museum, ACCESS moved to purchase an old furniture store, strategically located across the street from Dearborn City Hall, that had been boarded up for many years. Even before the building was purchased, an intensive discussion among ACCESS senior staff, ACCESS Cultural Arts Department and the ACCESS Board of Directors began to take place. What would be the nature of the museum, what would it focus on? What would its mission and goals be, what would it include (and exclude)? What kind of exhibits, programming and collections would it house?

Posing these kinds of questions made us realize the complexities and the challenges this undertaking would present. While we understood, in principle, the need for ethnically specific museums, including an Arab American National Museum, we also realized the problematic issues such institutions could present. Building a museum that focuses on Arab Americans and tells their story from their own perspective, if not planned and implemented carefully, could reinforce the view that Arab Americans are the "others" and not an integral part of the larger American story. We were also concerned that the presence of ethnic museums might help ghettoize minorities. In other words, would having our own institution that tells our own stories and presents our own culture provide a further justification for our exclusion from mainstream institutions?

By drawing similarities between Arab Americans and other immigrant groups' experiences, and by having Arab American stories presented within the larger American story, we hope that our visitors and readers realize that the Arab American story is actually the American story. It is the story of immigrants coming to this country to build a better life for themselves and their families.

We were also faced with the question of representation. Claiming that we needed to tell our story in our own voice assumes that Arab Americans have one voice and one story, which is of course not true. The challenge for us was to have the permanent exhibits reflect the complexity of the Arab American experience and represent Arab Americans in all their religious, national, professional, and lifestyle diversity; to create an institution that makes a fourth-generation Arab American Christian whose great-grandparents came from Syria and a newly arrived Muslim immigrant from Iraq feel that the museum tells both of their stories.

To address this issue, we developed exhibits that are inclusive of a wide range of personal stories. We traveled to a large number of cities and towns, met with new immigrants and third- and fourth-generation Arab Americans. We collected stories, artifacts, and historical documents from Arab Americans in every state. For example, we have in our exhibit artifacts sold by a Christian Lebanese peddler from Massachusetts, the trunk of a Yemeni farm worker living in California, the sewing kit of a Palestinian tailor in Michigan, and the prayer rug of a recent Iraqi refugee who settled in Arizona. These are just a few examples of the hundreds of stories collected and told by Arab Americans, their children and grandchildren. The Museum also has many recorded oral histories collected from families, libraries, and historical societies, including the Statue of Liberty-Ellis Island Foundation, that accompany the exhibits.

An additional challenge was the issue of constructing the Arab American identity; to decide who is and who is not an Arab American. For example, while some Lebanese Christians and Iraqi Chaldeans[3] do not identify themselves as Arab Americans, others do. How and who decides if these groups are to be included in the Museum? This is also the case of children from mixed marriages.

Our decision was simply to include those who define themselves as Arab Americans. Many Lebanese Christians were delighted to be included in the exhibit and responded positively to our calls for artifacts, photos and historical documents; a few did not, so we left them alone. The same was the case with children of mixed marriages. For Chaldean Americans we included some stories within the exhibits of those who identify themselves as both Arab and Chaldean; at the same time, we included a special section about Chaldean immigration, which included stories of those who identify themselves as Chaldean Iraqi Americans, rather than Arab Americans.

What complicated these issues even further is the fact that only one year after we started the planning process, the tragic events of September 11, 2001 took place. This made dealing with Arab identity and representation even more challenging. After September 11, Arab Americans felt under attack; fear and apprehension dominated our community. Many wanted to distance themselves from their Arab heritage and did not want to share their stories and experiences. Some of the people that I had planned to feature in the permanent exhibits contacted me, asking not to be included and to send back their artifacts. They expressed fear of having their stories in an "Arab" public place like the Museum. Some, especially new immigrants who were most targeted by hostilities, questioned the legitimacy and the sanity of building a museum under the existing situation.

While some of the fear faded away as time passed, some people continued to be apprehensive about being included in the Museum. However, when we look at the larger picture, the overall response of the Arab American community has been very encouraging. The hundreds of valuable artifacts, historical documents, photos and oral histories that are included in the three permanent exhibits featured in this book have been all donated by members of the community. We did not have to purchase a single item.

There was another challenge relating to people's willingness to have their stories included in the Museum's exhibits. Those who came from major metropolitan areas and had high levels of education were much more willing to share their stories with us and donate their artifacts and other belongings. On the other hand, many new immigrants, an important segment of the Arab American population, did not feel as comfortable being included. They were either concerned with basic needs like finding jobs, or they were simply afraid to tell their stories.

There was also the challenge of documenting Arab American contributions. While we realized the importance of including the contributions of certain individuals such as the late scholar Edward Said, journalist Helen Thomas, activist Ralph Nader, and surgeon Dr. Michael DeBakey, we felt that the contributions of ordinary people such as automobile, railroad and mine workers were just as important. A good example is an Arab American who served in the military; should the contributions of a person who had reached a high rank in the military such as George Joulwan or Alfred Naifeh be presented as more significant than that of foot soldiers who died on the field?

To address many of these challenges and answer these questions, we decided to consult with the Arab American community nationwide. As part of our planning strategy, we held consultation meetings in Michigan, and we visited Arab Americans in their cities and towns. The meetings brought together more than 50 scholars, museum professionals and community members to discuss the content of the Museum's permanent exhibits. The meetings were also instrumental in helping us establish relationships with Arab American communities around the country to facilitate research, collection of artifacts, and fundraising.

Additionally, for more than eight months in 2003, the museum team traveled around the country. We held meetings and focus groups in most cities that have large Arab American populations to assess the communities' vision and expectations of an Arab American National Museum. In these meetings, we posed similar questions about what they would like to see in an Arab American Museum, what would make it reflect their own experiences. Although we often heard contradictory points of view, there was some consistency and a clear consensus about what people expected from the Museum. People wanted to have the Museum reflect the beauty and richness of Arab architecture and to be modern at the same time, and to include a section about the contributions of the Arab World to world civilization. They wanted our exhibits to reflect the long presence of Arab Americans in this country, their diversity, their work, and contributions. Many mentioned the fact that Arab Americans had been part of the fabric of the U.S. since its inception and have fought and died for this country since the Revolutionary War. All these messages were critical in shaping our permanent exhibits and the way the exhibits tell our story.

The Arab American Story

The three thematic exhibits depicted in this publication occupy the entire second floor of the Museum. They employ a variety of multi-media activities, artifacts, film and video, music and audio and still photographs.

Coming to America examines the history of Arab American immigration starting in 1528, when the first known Arab, Al-Zamouri from Morocco, landed in the Gulf of Mexico as a slave. It takes us to the World's Fairs era when people came to the U.S. from Arab countries to participate in these fairs and ended up staying. Special attention is given to specific waves of immigration, especially the Great Migration period of 1880–1920, when Arab immigrants started coming in relatively large numbers. Most of these immigrants who came during the Great Migration were Christian villagers from Syria and Lebanon. In the post-World War II era, most of the immigrants were students and professionals who came from the urban middle class and were much more diverse in their national and religious background. The last wave of immigration, which started in the early 1970s and continues today, is made up mostly of war refugees from Palestine, Lebanon, and more recently from Iraq. The exhibit also explores Yemeni immigration and touches on emerging communities from North Africa, Sudan and Somalia. These waves are explored through the personal stories of Arab immigrants, reflecting the uniqueness of individual experiences as well as the broader shared experience.

Living in America focuses on the life of Arab Americans in the United States during different eras. Topics include family life, food, religion, activism and political involvement, institution-building, work and leisure. This exhibit takes our visitors through the experience of homesteading in South Dakota, peddling throughout the country, and owning and managing grocery stores and family businesses. It depicts the stories of Arab men and women who worked on automobile assembly lines, at shipyards, in coal mines, and in the garment industry, as well as Arab Americans professionals. It explores issues of discrimination and stereotyping. It also explores Arab Americans' diversity as well as their struggle to assimilate while retaining their culture.

Making an Impact tells the story of hundreds of Arab American individuals and organizations whose contributions have influenced our way of life. This exhibit is divided into several sections that include Arab American contributions in community organizations, politics, activism, science, academia, sports and the arts. It also includes a "Did You Know" section geared toward young people. Here our visitors learn about entertainer Danny Thomas, who founded St. Jude Children's Research Hospital, and Candace Lightner, founder of Mothers against Drunk Driving. They are introduced to world-renowned surgeon Dr. Michael DeBakey, consumer advocate and presidential candidate Ralph Nader, White House journalist Helen Thomas and NASA scientist Dr. Farouk El-Baz, among others.

Telling Our Story traces these stories and many others through individual voices and individual stories. It celebrates the presence and contributions of a community that have been so far unacknowledged. It brings to light this vitality of the Arab American community and gives it the recognition it well deserves.

[1] Dearborn is an adjacent suburb of Detroit. Its population is estimated at 100,000, one-third of which are Arab Americans.

[2] The Arab American National Museum is a project of the Arab Community Center for Economic and Social Services (ACCESS), a nonprofit organization committed to the development of the Arab American community in all aspects of its economic, social, and cultural life. Since its inception in 1971, ACCESS has grown from a small storefront office to an annual budget of over $14 million with 70 different programs, and a staff of 200.

[3] Chaldeans are a Christian Catholic minority from Iraq. While most speak Arabic, they do have their own language, Aramaic, the language believed to have been spoken by Jesus Christ. The majority of them live in Michigan and California.

The Development of Arab American Philanthropy

Maha Freij
CFO, ACCESS

When I first began in my capacity as Chief Financial Officer with ACCESS, I could not have envisioned that in such a brief period of time we would make the leaps and bounds that we have. By dedicating a significant and concerted effort aimed at institutional philanthropy we have exponentially grown in a small number of years. Although I have always maintained a vision driven by a focal point of growth and expansion, it's safe to say that the road we travel remains an unbeaten path.

ACCESS has always faced an immense accountability in ensuring that people of Arab descent realize their rightful and valued place in mainstream America. But with a sinking economy and unwarranted suspicion directed at Arab Americans across the country, the demand to create new traditions and customs in meeting the expanding needs of our growing numbers meant the added responsibility of improving our processes towards that objective.

It quickly became apparent to us that ACCESS must instill strategic philanthropic practices that would build and stabilize major institutions and then expand those efforts nationally and internationally. In February 2002, ACCESS confidently launched the Arab American Heritage Campaign with the Arab American National Museum (AANM) as its centerpiece.

The initial fundraising goal was $15 million, meant to spearhead the $20.6 million project targeting the building of the Museum ($12.8 million), a Community Health and Research Center ($3.3 million) and a Youth and Family Center ($4.5 million). In December 2002, ACCESS decided to increase the fundraising goal to $16 million. Having arrived at that goal well ahead of time, we immediately decided to seek the remaining $4.6 million to later avoid grappling with the question of long-term financing. By June 2006, we met and exceeded that goal as well.

During 2003, a project cost reallocation increased the funds for the AANM to $15.8 million, leaving $1.5 million as seed money for a future Youth and Family Center. Through the exposure to the long range rewards of philanthropy, prospective donors demonstrated a revived interest in the long-term success of the AANM. The possibility of realizing a tangible state-of-the-art institution fueled a robust increase in efforts, as well as donations, on the part of all partners and supporters to reach out and accomplish what had been unimaginable just years before. As a result, May 2002 marked the completion of a self-sufficient ACCESS Community Health and Research Center, allowing the Arab American Heritage Campaign to turn total focus on the creation of the very first Arab American National Museum.

Structuring the Heritage Campaign

In early 2001, an initial feasibility study indicated that the Arab American community at large was in fact poised for sweeping institutional advances. Zogby International, a well-respected polling research firm was then brought in to conduct a market analysis aimed at studying the community's readiness to move this endeavor forward. The Zoghby study results were overwhelmingly positive.

When the campaign finally went public in 2002, ACCESS hit the ground running. We had already reached 100% employee participation, meaning ACCESS staff raised $250,000 internally. With a total of $5.5 million, $2 million of that through a gift from the Ford Motor Company, the "silent" phase of the campaign was a resounding success.

Campaign Leadership & Structure

Campaign leadership consisted of a *Leadership Committee* responsible for overall goal setting and identifying and cultivating major individual and corporate prospective donors. Providing joint leadership of the campaign were Anthony Earley, CEO of DTE Energy, and Eugene Miller, Chairman and CEO of Comerica Incorporated. Esteemed individuals such as the Vice President of North American Business Operations at the Ford Motor Company, the International President of the United Auto Workers, and the CEO of The Henry Ford, along with ten other individuals, contributed greatly to this Committee. The Leadership Committee roster read like a Who's Who of metro Detroit business and civic leaders.

In late 2002, H.E. Bader Al-Dafa, Ambassador of the State of Qatar to the United States, joined the Leadership Committee. This addition widened our scope and abilities to cultivate and promote our visibility. As a result, we were able to add two International Honorary chairs, including the Secretary General of the Cooperation Council of the Gulf States and the Secretary General of the League of Arab States.

To capitalize on the potential for national contributions to the AANM project, in 2002 ACCESS formed a *National Advisory Board*, consisting of 68 members. The National Advisory Board represented Arab American national celebrities, community leaders, political figures, and intellectuals. As national ambassadors for the museum in their state, they promote membership, events and traveling exhibits, thus aiding the AANM in gaining national recognition.

Supporting the Leadership Committee was a *Campaign Oversight Team* consisting of five ACCESS executive staff and nine ACCESS Board Development Committee members. All members of this team had community ties that represented a diverse segment of the Arab population: Christians, Muslims, professionals, recent immigrants, and established or American-born families.

The *AANM Task Force Committee*, while largely concerned with project design and oversight, also directed some of the efforts in identifying prospective sources of financial support. It also represented the diversity of religious and ethnic backgrounds of all Arab Americans as well as brought forth individuals with museum backgrounds and cultural exchange experts.

One further campaign "division" worth mentioning is what can best be described as exemplary "corporate talent-sharing." The three corporations with the largest stake in our success — Comerica Incorporated, DTE Energy, and the Ford Motor Company — each designated a small group of executives to meet with Ismael Ahmed and me to review progress and brainstorm on the methodology to pursue prospects.

Implementing Processes

Defining the structure of the campaign helped us to move past the initial planning phase into the actual processes through which the campaign would solicit gifts on a face-to-face basis and implement broad-based fundraising plans.

Face-to-face Solicitations

The previously mentioned committees are directly involved in identifying, qualifying, cultivating, and soliciting new individual, corporate, foundation, and government prospects on the local, national, and international levels. Representatives of those committees work with at least 50 prospective major donors at any given time to develop a cultivation, stewardship, acknowledgement, and upgrade plan.

Broad-based Solicitations

During the initial phases of the campaign, our broad-based fundraising plan was executed through two telethons. Later we used the Kresge Challenge Grant to kick-start a direct mail program that encouraged $500 or more per donation to qualify for a permanent naming opportunity on the founders' wall.

In June 2004 we successfully met the Kresge challenge by reaching our overall goal of raising $16 million. After the opening of the AANM in May 2005, we again used the same technique to solicit memberships and expand its donor base. We instilled a tradition of offering foundership in the AANM for gifts of $1000 and more. We then went a step further by strongly encouraging those funds to be gifted to the AANM Endowment Fund.

In that same year, the community-at-large formed the *AANM Friends Committees* and independently embraced a commitment to support the museum and its goals. The most successful of these committees has been the Detroit Committee, which held its very first gala in April 2004. This first upscale and flawless effort generated $175,000 towards the Capital Campaign. Since the second AANM Museum Gala in 2005, the Detroit Committee has become a major force in supporting the operational needs of the Museum. We are now diligently working on replicating these successes through specific steps and aggressive fundraising goals in other cities across the nation.

Campaign Staffing

From 1998 to the fall of 2002, we managed to raise $11 million in capital funds without the support of an "official" development department. In mid-2002 it became clear that in order to further stabilize our collective vision we must create a Development Department.

Past Challenges, Future Focus

At the outset, this campaign was quite daunting considering the history of ACCESS in implementing strategic philanthropy. Throughout the first 30 years of our organization, we had managed only one $3.85 million capital campaign (Vision 2000), which was successfully completed in 1999. During times of overall economic duress, the diverse and talented yet philanthropically inexperienced Arab American leadership then set their sights on a goal four times greater.

By focusing on the future and a more politically and economically rooted Arab American community, we have raised almost $21 million in capital funds since 2001 and added about 3,000 new donors to our database. We have introduced a strong endowment dialogue to the Arab American agenda and as such have successfully raised and invested over $1 million in the museum endowment fund (first ever in the history of ACCESS). ACCESS has also upgraded the level of the single largest donation through the Arab American Heritage Campaign. For example, with the "Vision 2000" Capital Campaign, the single largest corporate donation was $400,000, but that increased fivefold to $2 million with the Arab American Heritage Campaign. The same can be said of foundation gifts going from $300,000 to $1.5 million for the Heritage Campaign. That pattern also holds true for individual donations that started at $50,000 and the single largest individual donation has now increased to $250,000.

ACCESS has only begun to scratch the surface of what we can collectively accomplish in expanding the scope and elevating the profile of Arab American giving. Philanthropy has made us realize the imperative responsibility we carry in today's society, to tell our own story, and then to build and sustain it. Harnessing this archetype of philanthropy has solidified our confidence and belief in that we as a people are capable of creating legacies and imprints for our children to follow and for future generations to replicate.

Our most pressing aim now is to significantly magnify this spirit and awareness of philanthropy among Arab Americans, thus empowering and motivating communities, institutions, and individuals around the nation to raise the bar and go beyond what has already now been accomplished.

Chapter One
Coming to America

Arab Americans have been coming to the United States for hundreds of years. Like other immigrants, they came seeking better lives for themselves and their families.

A Shared Identity

Arab Americans are among the many ethnic groups that make up the U.S. population. They trace their roots to the Arab world, which stretches from North Africa to West Asia. Arab Americans are just as diverse as the Arab world itself. They come from rural and urban areas in twenty-two different countries, practice different religions, work in a variety of fields, and have a range of educational backgrounds and political affiliations. Despite this diversity, Arab Americans have a shared sense of history, language, and cultural heritage.

Whereas the majority of the people who come from an Arab country identify themselves as Arab Americans, some might identify by their country of origin such as Syrian Americans or Palestinian Americans. Some might identify themselves by their ethnic backgrounds such as Chaldean Americans.

Arabs have been coming to the United States for hundreds of years. Like others, they came seeking better opportunities. The first significant number of immigrants came between 1880 and 1920. This slowed down drastically because of restrictive immigration laws passed after World War I. Since the 1970s, the number of Arab Americans has increased rapidly due to a change in these laws and because of wars and economic hardships in some Arab countries. It is estimated that by 2000 there were about 4.2 million Arab Americans.

Rababa

Gift of Suzan Samaan

Moroccan-born Zammouri, the first Arabic speaker who came to North America in 1528 as a slave, is also considered by some historians as the first African slave to arrive in North America.

The Very Early Immigrants

The first recorded Arabic speaker to come to North America was called "**Zammouri**," which in Arabic means "someone from Zammour." Zammour is the city in Morocco where he was born over five hundred years ago. He was sold into slavery and brought here, where he eventually became a famous healer and explorer. We know the story of his unique life from various chronicles.

Zammouri was probably captured in 1511, when Portugal invaded his city. He was then sold into slavery and his captors renamed him "Estebanico." After 16 years of captivity, Zammouri was taken to Florida as part of a Spanish expeditionary force. In 1528, he marched inland with three hundred other men, almost all of whom died. Zammouri, or Estebanico, is also considered by some historians as the first African American to come to North America.

Zammouri journeyed over six thousand miles between 1528 and 1536, trekking across the Southwest. Some historical accounts say that he and his

companions spent the first four years as prisoners of Native Americans until they were able to escape. Other Native Americans took them in and asked them to be medicine men. They were successful and their fame spread throughout the region. From this work, it is said that Zammouri learned six local dialects and was sought as a translator.

After experiencing slavery, the difficult passage to the Americas, and an eight-year trek across the country, Zammouri met an untimely death. In 1539, he was asked to be the chief guide for a Spanish expedition to explore new territory. On that trip, he became a victim in the struggle between Native Americans and European settlers. Zammouri was killed by Zunis in present-day New Mexico.

Historians recognize Zammouri's contributions to the exploration of the Southwest. The city of El Paso even commissioned artist John Houser to create a statue honoring him.

The Journey Out of Slavery

Zammouri may have been the first slave to come from an Arab country, but he was not the last. Many Arabs from North Africa were among the twelve to fifteen million slaves who arrived over the next four hundred years, many of whom ended up in the current U.S. states of Georgia and the Carolinas. Today, there are probably many Americans who have Arab slaves as their ancestors. Because slaves were given new names, their descendents are unable to trace themselves to their original families or hometowns.

Although it is difficult to estimate the number of slaves who came from current Arab countries such as Morocco, there are records that refer to the arrival in 1717 of Arabic-speaking Muslim slaves who would not eat pork. **Ben Ali** is among the few well-documented slaves. Like other prisoners on French vessels, he jumped ship in America. Later, he was a scout to the famous General Sumter during the Revolutionary War. Ben Ali changed his family name to Benenhaly. His sons later fought with the Confederate Army.

Omar Ibn Said was another Arabic-speaking slave. He had been trained in Quranic Arabic in his native land. John Owen, an early governor of North Carolina, decided to free Ibn Said on account of his apparent education. Ibn Said was later buried in the Owen family plot.

During the late 1700s, the South Carolina House of Representatives ruled that Moroccan Arabs living in the state should be treated according to the laws governing whites. The acknowledgment of Moroccan Arabs in the legal documents attests not only to the number of Moroccan Arabs in the South at the time, but also to the discriminatory nature of the laws, which privileged those classified as "whites."

Omar Ibn Said

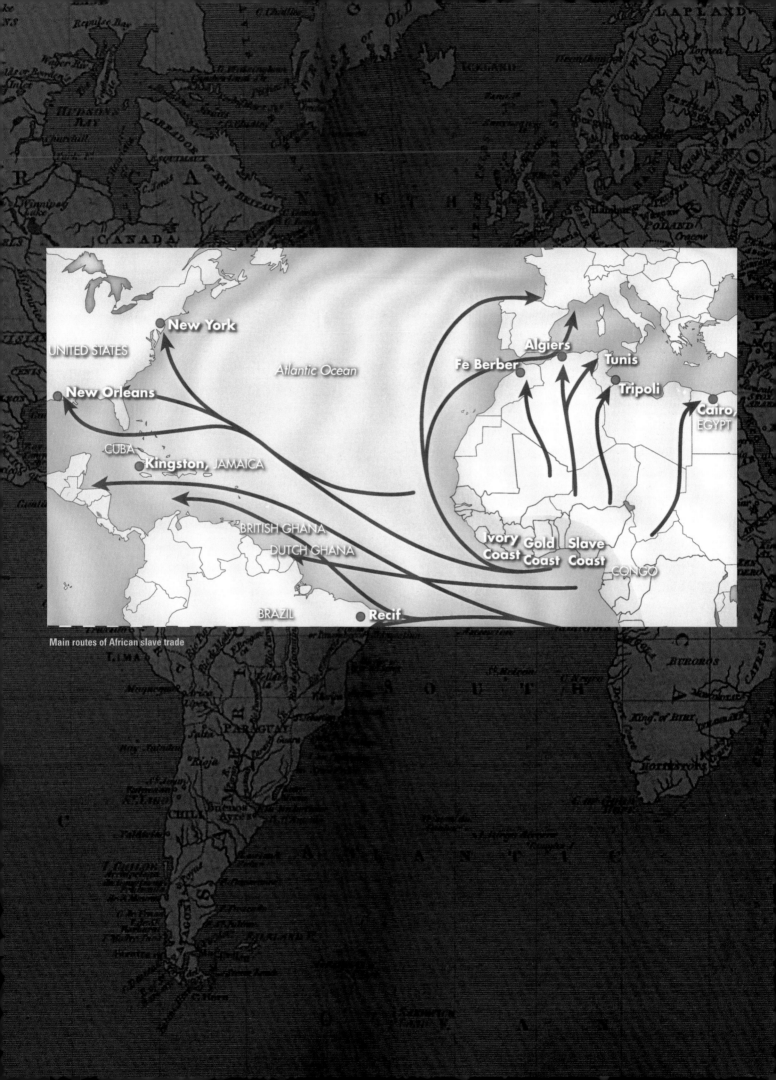

Main routes of African slave trade

Interaction of Trade and Religion

Interaction between the United States and the Arab world increased rapidly during the 1880s. Thanks to the new steamships, people were able to travel back and forth between the two regions quickly, safely, and cheaply. This interaction was not limited to migration from Arab countries to the United States, but also included American travel to Arab countries. A rise in affordable tourism prompted middle-class Americans to visit the Holy Land.

Many Christian missionaries also began traveling to Arab countries at this time to build churches, hospitals, and schools. As a result of missionary activities in the region, large numbers of Arabs came to learn about America and began to visit or immigrate here. The rapid urbanization and industrialization occurring in mid-nineteenth century America further propelled the development of transatlantic trade routes and increased Arab migration to the United States.

American tourists arriving in the Holy Land, c. 1860

The American University of Beirut (AUB) was established in 1866 as the American Syrian Protestant College. Since Beirut was a major city port, the creation of AUB exemplified the growing importance of commercial, economic, and cultural interaction between the United States and Greater Syria at the turn of the century. AUB is now one of the foremost universities in the Arab world and continues to attract a large number of foreign students, including Americans.

Antonius Bishellany was among the early travelers who came to the United States after meeting American missionaries and tourists. Originally from a village in Greater Syria (which included modern day Syria, Lebanon, Jordan, Palestine, and Israel), Bishellany was born a Maronite Catholic and converted to Protestantism—an act for which he was shunned by his community. He came to the United States in 1854, bringing with him the names and addresses of Americans he had met while working as a tour guide in Beirut. Bishellany's intention was to study in the United States and then return to his country to become a Protestant missionary.

After arriving at the port in East Boston, he soon made his way to New York City where he is reported to have worked as a butler. He then received a scholarship to study at the Amenia Seminary in upstate New York in return for giving Arabic lessons to missionaries preparing to go to the Arab world. Before he could finish his studies, he became ill and died from tuberculosis. Bishellany is buried with a Bible in Greenwood Cemetery in New York City.

American University of Beirut

Antonius Bishellany and his Bible

Boston Harbor, c. 1850s

Hadj Ali is another well-known Arab who came from Syria to America in the nineteenth century. He was actually brought by Major Henry Wayne, upon the recommendation of Secretary of War Jefferson Davis following the war with Mexico in the 1840s.

At the end of the war, the United States acquired from Mexico the current state of Arizona. With this acquisition, crossing the desert during the Gold Rush presented an opportunity and a challenge. Before the railroad connected the East and West Coasts, crossing the country depended on horses, mules, and oxen, animals that required plenty of water. The water scarcity in the Southwest prompted Secretary of War Jefferson Davis to propose a Camel Military Corps to Congress. The plan was to utilize the camels to help build and supply a wagon route from Texas to California. Hadj Ali was brought to America to train camels and help run the famous Camel Corps.

The soldiers called him "Hi Jolly" because they could not pronounce his name. In 1880, he became a citizen with the name Philip Tedro. The Arizona State Highway Department erected a monument to him over his gravesite in 1935.

Bell worn around the neck of each camel of the Camel Military Corps

Loading a camel at the U.S. Army headquarters' warehouse in Wilmington, California for a trip to an Arizona fort, c.1860

Monument to Hadj Ali, Quartzite, Arizona, 1935

THE LAST CAMP OF
HI JOLLY
BORN SOMEWHERE IN SYRIA
ABOUT 1828
DIED AT QUARTZSITE
DECEMBER 16 1902
CAME TO THIS COUNTRY
FEBRUARY 10 1856
CAMELDRIVER — PACKER
SCOUT — OVER THIRTY
YEARS A FAITHFUL AID
TO THE U.S. GOVERNMENT

Boutros Holwey traveled to the U.S. for the World's Columbian Exposition in 1893 as a representative of Egypt. A Syrian, Holwey had built a reputable inlaid mosaic palace made up of more than two million pieces which was to be exhibited at the Exposition. After the fair concluded, Holwey stayed in the United States, and, according to some accounts, traveled to Mexico to train followers of the revolutionary leader Pancho Villa in swordsmanship.

The World's Fairs also prompted some to come from various Arab countries to the United States. Modeled after the World's Fairs in Europe, the 1876 Philadelphia Centennial Exposition and the 1893 Chicago Exposition sought to celebrate America's modernity and invited countries from around the world to exhibit their products and cultures. These fairs increased cultural and economic interests between America and the rest of the world.

The Promotion Department of the United States government devised extensive recruitment campaigns, sending agents to visit different countries and issuing invitations to consuls and diplomats. Individuals who spoke English were encouraged to come and were offered higher wages. The fairs attracted a number of Arabs from Egypt, Syria, Lebanon, Morocco, Tunisia, and Algeria, including merchants who heard of American interest in luxury items. Many Arabs stayed and settled in the United States.

Cairo, Jan 29, 1874

Hon. A. F. Goshorn
Director General
U.S. Centennial Exhibition
Philadelphia

Sir,

I have the honor to address you on the subject of the approaching Centennial Exhibition to be held in 1876, with the object of securing, if possible, the representation of Egypt therein.

I am officially informed that the government of the United States is not authorized by the act of Congress on the subject, to issue invitations to other governments to participate in the Exhibition and that no such invitations have been given.

I presume it is desirable that Egypt should be properly represented on that occasion. A choice and artistic collection of her products, costumes, architecture and antiquities together with a good representation of her customs, manners, people and laws would form an interesting and picturesque feature of the great Exhibition, the complete success of which should be the desire and endeavor of every American.

I feel confident that His Highness the Khedive would be gratified to receive an official invitation to participate in the Exhibition and he would undoubtedly exert himself to have Egypt represented in a manner creditable to herself and satisfactory to the patrons of the Exhibition.

I submit this matter to your consideration and I will be most happy to be the means of conveying to the Khedive any communication on the subject, or you may decide if wise to transmit and in furthering the interest of the Exhibition at all times.

I am, sir,
Very respectfully,
Your indebted servant,
R. Beardsley
U.S. Agent Consul General

Classifying Arabs

Today, we think of "race" or "ethnicity" as Black, White, Latino, or Asian. But both race and ethnicity are cultural classifications that had changed over time. Over the years, immigration officials classified people in different ways, according to physical characteristics, national origin, or religion.

During the years of the Great Migration, 1880–1924, it was especially difficult to classify Arabs because they came from both African and Asian countries. They also did not fit any physical characteristics that were used to classify race because their features, including skin color and hair texture, varied widely. Until 1899, Arabs were classified as Greeks, Armenians, and Turks. Later, they were sometimes categorized as Ottoman, African, Asian, White, or European. Because of these changing classifications, we cannot always tell from government records if an immigrant was Arab.

Before Ellis Island

When people think about the Great Migration, they immediately think of Ellis Island. But before Ellis Island, there was Castle Garden, which is located on the southern tip of Manhattan. This former military fort opened in 1855 as a receiving station for immigrants. For the next 35 years, more than eight million people passed through Castle Garden; many were from Arab countries. In 1897, the buildings at Castle Garden were destroyed by a fire, as were all records going back to 1855. Therefore, of the many Arabs who came through Castle Garden, we only know of those whose stories were passed down through families, newspapers, or other public records.

The **Arbeelys** of Damascus were the first recorded Arab family to come to the United States with the intention of becoming citizens. Dr. Joseph Arbeely, his wife, six sons, and niece arrived in New York on August 20, 1878. A photograph of the Arbeely family appeared in a newspaper with the caption, "Syrians in America." Due to Dr. Arbeely's prominent reputation as a professor, the press welcomed the family with open arms. Two of Dr. Arbeely's sons, Najeeb and Ibrahim, went on to establish the first Arabic newspaper in America, *The Star of America*, in 1892.

The Arbeely family

146. Castle Garden & Bay. N.Y.

The Great Migration

During the Great Migration (1880–1924), more than 20 million immigrants entered the United States. Approximately 95,000 of these immigrants were from Greater Syria (present-day Syria, Lebanon, Jordan, Palestine, and Israel). Because of the growing numbers of Arab immigrants in that period, Najeeb Arbeely was hired by the immigration officials as a facilitator and interpreter. By 1924 the number of Arabs living in the United States was estimated at 200,000.

At the time of the Great Migration, the majority of Arab countries were colonized by the Ottoman Empire, which ruled the Arab world from 1500–1917. By the 1850s, the Empire had lost much of its strength and was facing rapid political and economic decline. For example, the Ottomans increased taxes and forced Christians and Jews—previously exempt—to serve alongside Muslims in the military. Meanwhile, the silk and vineyard industries in Lebanon began to collapse around the end of the nineteenth century. World War I (1914–1917) brought widespread famine and poverty to the region. This combination of factors led many to come to the United States.

The majority of Arabs that came at this time were Lebanese/Syrian Christians. Many settled in cities such as New York, Boston, and Detroit, where textile, peddling, and automotive industries promised employment. As time passed, families brought their relatives over, and communities were established that helped new arrivals.

Moses (Dewan) Bounassar and his wife (Miriam) Mansour Dahdooh became Michael and Mary Moses when they arrived at Ellis Island from Hasbaya al Metn, Lebanon

Forzley family portrait

Bashara Khalil Forzley
dancing at the wedding of
his youngest child

"Don't Forget Your Folks at Home"

The story of **Bashara Khalil Forzley** (B.K.) is typical of many Arabs who immigrated to the United States during the Great Migration. He came to find work to support his family back home. Upon arrival, other relatives who had already immigrated here helped him settle and find work. Later, B.K. brought other members of his family to the United States. The process of bringing relatives and family members one after the other is known as "chain migration."

B.K. was born in 1883 in Karhoun, Lebanon. As he got older, his father was unable to work the family farm and when B.K. turned 14 years old, his mother sent him to America to find work. B.K.'s cousin had already immigrated to the United States and settled in Worcester, Massachusetts. Upon B.K.'s departure his mother pinned his cousin's address to his jacket. As he set off from Beirut in 1897, his mother gave him this advice, "Always associate yourself with people who are your elders, do not indulge in liquor, smoking, dating, or partying, and do not forget your folks at home. If you live and succeed we also will succeed by our manifested happiness."

As soon as B.K. arrived in Massachusetts, his cousin, who owned a dry goods store, sent him to work as a peddler. After work, B.K. learned English so that he could receive his citizenship and a peddling license. In 1905, he became a U.S. citizen.

That same year, B.K. sent for his older brother Abraham to join him. In 1908, he went back and married Almaza, whose parents were already in America. The two sailed to New York and arrived at Ellis Island.

B.K. and Almaza settled in Worcester among the Syrian community. They named their son "Victor" after the American victory in World War I. B.K. stayed in touch with his family in Lebanon and visited them several times. He also donated generously to his native village of Karhoun. In 1958, B.K. published his autobiography in English.

"In my wakefulness, during the day as I go about doing my daily chores, walk in the streets of New York, listening to the din of speeding trains, and of trams on the ground and above ground, and the sirens of ships and the deafening of people piercing my ears, and the bustle of streetcars and carriages and the glitter.... I only come around soaring in the skies of Jerusalem, over the school, over the house that I love, and often over Artas and Kalona, Ein Karem, and Beit Jala. And when I go to sleep it is not because I am sleepy, but because I wait for slumber to overtake me. Not to sleep but to get rid of the pains of wakefulness, hoping to get rid of my heaviness, and hoping to get rid of my body—to leave it in America, and to fly in dreams to Jerusalem."

— Khalil Sakakini

Missing Home

About one-third of the estimated forty million people who came to the United States between 1830 and 1930 returned home. **Khalil Sakakini**, a prominent intellectual and educator from Palestine, was among them. He came to the United States in 1907 hoping to find work, save some money, and pay off his debts before getting married to his beloved Sultana Abdo, whom he left behind in Jerusalem. Khalil was planning to join his brother who had already immigrated to the United States and settled in Philadelphia. Unfortunately, when he arrived, he found the country in an economic recession and his brother was having a hard time finding employment. He decided to stay in Brooklyn, where he became involved with the cultural and intellectual community of Arab Americans, and began writing for the journal, *al-Jamia*.

His writings often contrasted "the coldness of New York's modernity and capitalism with the intimacy and tradition of Jerusalem."

After one year in the United States, Khalil returned to Palestine. He married Sultana Abdo four years later, and soon became a radical innovator of the education system in Palestine. To honor him and acknowledge his contributions, the Sakakini Cultural Centre, a nonprofit organization for the preservation and promotion of Palestinian culture, was founded in Ramallah, Palestine, in 1996.

In 2003 the Sakakini Cultural Center published 3,400 pages of Khalil's handwritten memories.

Nora Roum while seven months pregnant

Nora's daughter, Elsie, was born on
Ellis Island on December 10, 1937

Women: Independent and Strong

The first Arab immigrants to come during the Great Migration were mostly men. By the beginning of the 1900s, however, one-third of Arab immigrants were women. While many had been sent for by a male relative, a number of women, both married and single, traveled to the United States alone. Most of these women knew at least a friend or a relative who could help them upon arrival.

Many women traveled in extremely difficult situations. **Nora Roum** arrived at Ellis Island from Syria seven months pregnant and was detained for observation because of an eye condition. She did not like the hospital's food and her uncle brought her some Arabic food—cheese, olives, and pita bread. Nora placed them in a cabinet beside her bed. During the night, she became hungry and opened the cabinet only to find a rat feasting on her food. Nora screamed in fright and soon went into labor. Her baby was named Elsie, for the island on which she was born.

Saleemie Yazigie (1868–1944) was among these Arab women who came to the United States with only one of her daughters. She planned to earn enough money to send for her husband and four daughters, whom she had left behind in Lebanon.

Like many Arabs, Saleemie learned about America from missionaries in Beirut. As an English teacher, she was fascinated with America and wanted to immigrate, but her husband George was reluctant to leave. He changed his mind later when a fire killed the horses that he raised, and the family faced financial difficulties. Saleemie decided to go to America with her oldest daughter, and they arrived in New York in 1902. From New York they went to Massachusetts, where she had a relative. Like many other Arab women, they worked in a hosiery mill. Five years later, Saleemie sent for the rest of her family and they were reunited on Ellis Island. Due to an eye ailment, George was not permitted to enter the country and was sent back. Tragically, he died in Naples on the return trip to Syria.

Through Central and South America

Not all Arab immigrants came to the United States through New York or Boston; many came through Central and Latin America. Some immigrants who were denied entry to the United States, often for medical reasons, went to Mexico, and later came to the United States. Others emigrated first to Latin America and then came to the United States to join relatives or find work. Many of the Arab immigrants who came through Central and South America settled in Texas, Florida, or southern California.

By the early 1900s, many Arabs came to Texas via Mexico. El Paso directories of the time list Spanish first names with Arabic last names. The high number of Arab immigrants prompted the El Paso Immigration Service to hire two Syrian interpreters—Salim Mattar and Esau Malooly.

Mansour Nahra was one of those Arabs who came to the United States via Central America. On his way to the United States, he went through Mexico, where he joined the Mexican Revolution and met Pancho Villa. Mansour once explained to his grandchildren that he did this because as a Lebanese he had a duty to help those in trouble. After the revolution, he continued on to California with a stack of pesos. Although the pesos were not worth much in California, Mansour kept them and passed them down to his grandchildren. Mansour went on to open a furniture store in the Hispanic section of Los Angeles.

Dieb and his wife, Adelia

Annette and Hedy Meda

Michel Laham

Michel Nicolas Laham was born in Rashaya al-Wadi in southern Lebanon in the 1870s. During World War I, he owned a store in Damascus that specialized in luxury fabrics. An Orthodox Christian with strong religious ties to Czarist Russia, Michel invested all his savings in Russian rubles. When the Bolshevik revolution occurred, the Russian currency lost its value, and Michel lost all his savings.

In 1919, Michel decided to emigrate with his family to Haiti. In the 1930s, his sons Nicolas and Fawzy immigrated to the United States, settling in Jacksonville, Florida.

Dieb Karam

Influenced by stories of other immigrants who returned to the village, Dieb Karam, his wife, and seven other young men decided to leave for America in 1907. On the day of their departure, they left the village on foot. Dieb's father, Becos Elias Karam, followed slowly behind, calling out to his son, "Dieb, call my name," and Dieb called back, "Papa, Papa, I hear you." As they drifted out of sight he yelled, "Dieb call my name one more time, for I know this will be the last time I will hear your voice." When the group was out of sight and Becos could no longer hear his son's voice, he fell to the ground and wept. That was the last time he saw his son or heard his voice.

Sad departures like this were repeated thousands of times during the turn of the twentieth century as the sons and daughters of many immigrants left their native land for a new life.

Annette Meda

Mackoul Meda left Ferouzi, Syria and came to the United States around 1919. He worked, saved money, returned to Syria, and married Annette Abdelnour. Soon they had a daughter whom they named Hedy. Because Mackoul was not yet an American citizen, he was unable to bring his wife and daughter with him when he returned to the United States.

Annette tried to join her husband in Michigan by entering the United States from Mexico. The journey was long and hard: a three-month stay in Marseilles, France, then on to Cuba and then Mexico. As Annie and her daughter traveled by donkey across the Rio Grande, the guide abandoned them in the desert. They followed a light in the distance where someone helped them reach St. Louis, Missouri. In Cincinnati, Ohio relatives helped them reach Detroit, Michigan where they were reunited with Mackoul.

The Titanic

There were one hundred fifty-four Arabs on the Titanic, twenty-nine of whom survived the wreck: four men, twenty women, and five children. This famous ship struck an iceberg while crossing the Atlantic in 1912. More than half of the crew and passengers died.

One of the survivors was Anna Yousef, a woman from the small Lebanese village of Tibnin. Anna was traveling on the Titanic with her two children. She was trying to join her husband Darwin Toma and his brother, who had been working in Dowagiac, Michigan for seven years.

When the iceberg hit, Anna's hand was slammed in a door. Unaware that the ship would sink, she went to the infirmary to tend to her hand. After she realized what was happening, she quickly left the infirmary and found her two children. After receiving three life jackets, they were helped onto a lifeboat. Anna covered her children

with a coat so that they would not see the horrific scene of the Titanic sinking. At dawn, their boat was rescued.

Anna and her children made it to Michigan. She lived to be 91 years old. Her grandson, Joseph Thomas, preserved her story in his book, *Grandma Survived the Titanic*.

Anna Yousef Thomas and family. Anna is seated in white

Closing the Gates

Arabs were among the millions of people who came to the United States during the Great Migration. These immigrants provided the labor that helped transform this country from a semi-agricultural society into one of the world's most advanced industrial powers.

As the number of immigrants grew after the turn of the twentieth century, these communities began to face hostility from the Euro-Americans who had come before them. The new immigrants were often discriminated against and stereotyped because of their different cultural and socioeconomic backgrounds. With the economic recession during the early twentieth century, immigrants were often perceived as taking jobs away from "Americans." Increasing anti-immigrant sentiment in popular culture and among politicians eventually led to legislation that restricted immigration from countries that were not in Northern or Western Europe.

Because Greater Syria (which includes modern-day Syria, Lebanon, Jordan, Palestine, and Israel) is in western Asia, some district courts questioned whether Syrians should be considered as part of the "Yellow Race" and thus excluded from citizenship under the Asian Exclusion Act of 1882. Later, shortly before World War I, the courts ruled that Syrians were not part of the "Yellow Race" and were therefore eligible for citizenship. This case highlights the difficulties of racial classification of Arabs.

Between 1917 and 1924, the U.S. Congress passed a number of laws restricting Arab immigration. The 1917 Immigration Act imposed a literacy requirement and excluded people coming from most of Asia and the Pacific Islands. The 1921 Quota Act and the Immigration Act of 1924 established a quota system that placed greater restrictions on immigrants from all countries except for Northern and Western Europe.

The New Immigrants: Exiles and Refugees

After World War I, Palestinians became a significant segment of Arab immigration to the United States. The main reasons were the British occupation of Palestine and the subsequent creation of the State of Israel. These related events created thousands of Palestinian refugees and exiles who were dispersed throughout the world. The events also created the seeds of the current Arab-Israeli conflict.

During World War I, the Arab governments sided with the Allies: Britain, France, Russia, and the United States. They joined the fight against the Central Powers led by Austria-Hungary, the German Empire, Bulgaria and the Ottoman Empire. Britain and France had promised to help the Arabs gain independence from the Ottomans in return for their support. Despite this promise, Britain and France signed a secret document dividing up Arab land. France took control of Syria and Lebanon and Britain established a mandate to rule Iraq, Jordan, and Palestine. This was the famous Sykes-Picot Agreement (1916), which divided Greater Syria into the countries that we know today (Syria, Lebanon, Jordan, and Palestine).

A year later, Britain issued the Balfour Declaration (1917), which promised support for a Jewish homeland in Palestine. Subsequently, European Jews began to emigrate there. Palestinians feared that they would never gain freedom from the British and that a Jewish state would end their quest for independence. The political and economic unrest led many Palestinians to come to the United States. For the first time, during the 1930s, Palestinian immigration to the United States exceeded that of the Syrians and Lebanese.

Nowhere to Go

The 1948 creation of the State of Israel displaced a large number of Palestinians from their homes. The United Nations estimates that during 1949–1950 there were 726,000 to 914,000 registered refugees, most of whom were forced to leave their homes in Palestine and go to neighboring Arab countries. Others went to Europe, Australia, and Canada. In 1953, the U.S. Congress passed the Refugee Relief Act, allowing two thousand Palestinian families to immigrate. Another 985 were allowed to immigrate between 1958 and 1963.

Ahmad and his family

Ahmad Essa Ibrahim was born in Jimsu, Palestine in 1922. In 1948, he and his family were forced to leave their home and farmlands following the declaration of the State of Israel. They left behind their wheat mill and groves of fruit and olives and fled to the West Bank, where they lived in a tent near Ramallah. As the weather grew cold, they moved from town to town seeking shelter and work.

Because of these hardships, Ahmad decided to immigrate to America. His wife Aisha had a cousin in Brooklyn who agreed to sponsor Ahmad as part of the Refugee Relief Act of 1953. Aisha sold her jewelry to pay for her husband's travel to America, except for a necklace she had received as a wedding gift. She sent the necklace with Ahmad as a gift for her cousin's wife in appreciation of their help.

After arriving in Manhattan, Ahmad took a taxi to the Brooklyn home of Moussa, his wife's cousin. Moussa and his wife helped him start his work as a peddler of linens, tapestries, and blankets. Ahmad worked hard to support himself and send money to his family back home.

In 1962, Ahmad returned to his family for ten months and brought two of his children back to the United States with him. In 1966, the whole family reunited in America. All of Ahmad and Aisha's children went on to receive advanced degrees; four of them became medical doctors.

Above: Ahmed Ibrahim note book which he brought with him when he came to the U.S in 1953. It has his wife's cousin's address in Manhattan where he was planning to go upon his arrival.
Center: 1946 Palestinian coin, the word Palestine written in Arabic, English and Hebrew
Left: Pre-1948. Key of a home in Palestine

Girard Place
Maplewood, New Jersey
January 13th, 1950

Department of State
Office of African and Near Eastern Affairs
Washington 25, D.C.

Gentlemen:

I have before me your letter of October 13, 1949. By this time I hope you have accomplished something regarding the two questions which I have placed before you.

Again I should like to draw your attention to the pertinent fact that the settlement of my property issue should not come under the heading of "Arab Refugees." I am not an Arab refugee, but an American citizen. I am not involved in the Jewish-Arab war as I left Palestine in October, 1944; i.e., four years before the termination of the British mandate. My case, therefore, should be handled independently of any Arab-Jewish complications.

I have good reason to believe that my orange grove is ruined. It is in Israeli territory and, therefore, the Israeli authorities should be responsible for it.

As an American citizen resident in the United States, to whom should I turn for redress except to you? I cannot go on forever leaving this vital matter to circumstances and to the mercy of the Israeli Government. I am willing to sell the property for the proper price as I have no intention of ever living in Israel. I claim damages for whatever harm befell the property. It is now that I need the money as I have a boy in college and two girls in high school.

It is my hope that you will take immediate and effective action as you are the only agency that can produce results.

Thank you in advance,
Sincerely yours,

Khalil Totah

Sana and Amer

Amer and Sana

Musician Amer Kadaj and his wife Sana bid farewell to Palestine in 1947. They had originally planned to stay in America only a few months, but because of war in Palestine, they were unable to return. Over the next decade, the Kadaj's developed a successful musical career in Detroit and were cherished by Arab Americans throughout the United States.

Sana and Amer (at right)

The Brain Drain

The next wave of Arab immigration to the United States occurred in the post-World War II period. This wave was more diverse than earlier ones. Early Arab immigrants were mostly Syrian and Lebanese Christians from rural backgrounds and had limited formal education. This wave included both Christians and Muslims who came from various Arab countries. Many of them came from urban middle-class backgrounds and enjoyed high levels of education.

This wave of immigration came at a time when the United States was trying to recruit highly educated people from around the world in order to enhance its status as a technological superpower. Many of the students, who came with the intention of returning to their home countries after graduation, remained here because of the employment opportunities provided for them. Although Arab professionals had helped build a strong post-war America, their immigration resulted in a "brain drain" from the Arab world, a loss of the most skilled and educated.

Coming from newly independent Arab countries, these Arab students and professionals had a strong sense of the Arab identity and were politically active. They quickly became involved in the American political system, and revived the Arab identity among earlier immigrants.

Iraq: Dr. Hussam A. Fadhli

As a boy growing up in Baghdad, Hussam Fadhli was torn between his interest in the arts and his proficiency in science. His desire to become a physician won. He moved to the United States in 1957 to complete his medical post-graduate studies, and later opened a private practice in Texas. In 1969, he became the first surgeon to perform an open-heart surgery in southeast Texas.

Dr. Fadhli could not abandon his artistic interests. In watching his wife, Bridgette, with her Arabian horses, he developed a desire to translate the beauty and spirit of the horses into sculpture. A self-taught artist, Dr. Fadhli's work has been displayed at the 2002 Olympic Winter Games and is in the collection of the Bush Presidential Library.

Hussam often uses his old medical instruments in creating his work and says that the two disciplines are not that different. "Surgery is the transformation of mental ideas into an operation. Sculpting is the transformation of ideas into the medium you are using."

Presenting a diploma in wildlife biology to his son Gibran Michael Suleiman, 1997 (above). Upon receiving his Ph.D. from the University of Wisconsin, 1965 (left)

Laila at her wedding, held at the Islamic Center in Washington, D.C., 1959

Palestine: Michael Suleiman

Michael Suleiman is another Arab American who originally came to this country as a student. As a Palestinian refugee in Jordan, he had limited opportunities to gain a college education except by scholarship. Michael's high school principal suggested that he contact an American Presbyterian minister who had previously lived in Jordan. The minister, Oliver Page, wrote Michael a letter of sponsorship and suggested he attend Bradley University near where he lived in Illinois. Page met the young student at the pier in New York City and introduced him to life in America. After receiving his Ph.D. from the University of Wisconsin, Madison, Michael was awarded a teaching position at Kansas State University in Manhattan, where he has become a prominent scholar of Arab American culture and history.

Egypt: Laila Russell

Laila Russell was one of the many Arabs who originally came to the United States to pursue an advanced degree. Born in Cairo, Egypt, Laila attained a Bachelor's degree in 1953. Three years later, she was awarded a Fulbright scholarship and a grant from the Egyptian government to study rural education at an American university of her choice. She went on to obtain a Ph.D. in Education from the University of Wisconsin, Madison. Afterwards, Laila and her family moved back to Egypt. In 1969, she took a position at Shaw University, North Carolina, where she remained until her retirement in 2000.

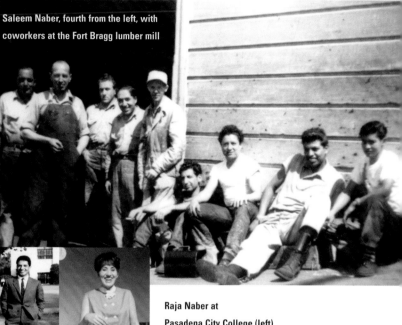

Saleem Naber, fourth from the left, with coworkers at the Fort Bragg lumber mill

Raja Naber at
Pasadena City College (left)
Evelyn Naber (right)

Syria: Bassam Barazi

Bassam Barazi was born in Hama, Syria on June 3, 1942. After he graduated from high school in 1962, he traveled to Texas where his cousin lived and enrolled in the University of Texas in Austin. As with many other students, Bassam had originally planned to return to Syria after finishing his Bachelor's degree. Because of the unstable political and economic situation at home at the time, he decided to stay in America. Upon graduating with a degree in Civil Engineering in January of 1968, Bassam moved to Houston where he found a job with the Texas Highway Department. He became a naturalized citizen of the United States in 1973. Bassam and his family settled in Houston, where there is a large Syrian professional community.

Jordan: The Naber Family

The Naber family is a typical example of chain migration. The first person of the Naber family to immigrate to the United States was Saleem Naber, who came in 1950 as a student at the University of California in Berkeley. They eventually settled with their four children in southern California. Saleem became president of Western Gear, an engineering company that built the Seattle Space Needle.

In 1953, Saleem's brother, Suleiman, came to the United States to attend San Francisco State University, California. Three additional brothers, Salem, Raja, and Yacoub, came to the United States in 1960. Their sister, Evelyn Naber, arrived in 1969. Today, the entire family lives in the San Francisco area.

Change in Consciousness

In the 1960s, Arabs in the United States became more conscious of their Arab identity due to political struggles here and abroad. The primary reasons for this change in consciousness were the nationalist movements in developing countries, including the Arab world, and the Civil Rights movement in the United States.

In the Arab world, the 1950s and 1960s witnessed a strong rise in Arab nationalism. This new era of nationalism was led by the popular Egyptian president Gamal Abdel Nasser. People around the world revered him for standing up to the colonial powers and for his solidarity with formerly colonized countries. Abdel Nasser helped unite North African Arabs with sub-Saharan Africans in the Organization of African Unity. He co-organized the Non-Aligned Movement of developing countries, which sought liberation from Western dominance. Arabs everywhere, including those in the United States, began to see their struggle as linked with others around the world.

This strong sense of Arab identity was brought to the United States by students and professionals who had participated in nationalist movements in the Arab world. As a result, many Arabs here began to identify as "Arab Americans," rather than as people of a particular country or village. The Civil Rights movement also spurred political activism. Like African Americans and Native Americans, Arab Americans began to assert their rights.

Activist Aliya Hassan and a delegation of Arab and African Americans meet with Gamal Abdel Nasser in Egypt

A first generation Arab American, **Kay Elder** (1926–2003) was an icon in the South End of Dearborn, Michigan, where she settled with her family in 1954.

Through her fighting spirit and pursuit of human rights, the long-time activist "Hajja" gained local and national respect. In the 1960s she, along with other members of her community, stood in front of bulldozers to stop the demolition of homes during the City of Dearborn's attempts to transform the South End residential neighborhood into an industrial area.

In 1972 she returned with her family to her hometown Beit Hanina in Palestine. There she was nicknamed "Um Al Khair" ("Mother of Good Deeds"), as she touched the lives of thousands of Palestinian refugees and orphans

By assuming nontraditional roles of activist, entrepreneur, humanitarian, and philanthropist, Kay Elder was a pioneer in the advancement of women both here and in Palestine.

Mahfoud Bennoune during the Algerian Revolution

Mahfoud Bennoune was born in Algeria in 1939. In 1955, he joined the Algerian Army of National Liberation (ALN), which fought for freedom from France during the Algerian War for Independence. Captured during a mission in Algiers, he served for five years as a prisoner of war, and suffered significant hearing loss in one ear as a result of being tortured.

In 1967, Bennoune immigrated to the United States, where he earned a Ph.D. in Anthropology from the University of Michigan, although he did not have a high school diploma.

Yemeni Immigration

Yemeni immigration to the United States has a long history. Yemeni men have been leaving their country for centuries to find work in other parts of the world and support their families back home. By 1890, there was a small number of Yemenis in America and a handful served in the U.S. military during World War I. After World War II, some came to the United States through Vietnam, where they had worked in a variety of trades. It was easier to acquire a U.S. visa from Vietnam than from Yemen.

The number of Yemeni immigrants increased rapidly after the abolishment of the quota system in 1965. Many Yemenis have worked on farms in California, in automobile factories in Michigan, and in steel plants in New York. Others have opened small businesses.

Earlier immigrants were mostly men who intended to work here temporarily and return home. Since the early 1970s, however, many began bringing their families. Today, there are many Yemeni Americans born in the United States.

Nagi Daifallah came to the United States from Yemen looking for a better life. He found employment in the grape fields in California's Central Valley, where many immigrants from Yemen worked. He quickly learned Spanish and English, which enabled him to mediate between workers within the United Farm Workers Union. Soon he became a leader in the fight to improve working conditions.

When thousands of grape workers went on strike for fair wages and better working conditions in the summer of 1973, Nagi was among them. During these strikes, local police arrested more than 3,500 workers and their families, and hundreds were beaten. On August 15, 1973, at the age of 24, Nagi Daifallah was beaten to death by a deputy sheriff. Today, thousands of farmworkers commemorate and honor the Arab American leader, Nagi Daifallah.

MERIP Reports 34. 1975. The cover of this issue memorializes activist Naji Daifallah, a union interpreter killed by a county sheriff in 1973. An ACLU spokesman said of Daifallah, "He believed that Filipinos, Chicanos, and Yemenis had enough dignity to stand together."

Straw hat. Circa 1980. Worn by Mohamed Abdallah while working in the fields. Below: Employment identification card. Circa 1973

Born in a small village in Yemen, **Mohamed Abdallah** lost his parents as a young child. When he was a teenager, he obtained a visa to the United States. He arrived with only $7, an address of a Yemeni coffee shop, and no knowledge of English.

Arriving at the coffee shop, Mohamed met several Yemenis. One generously gave him a $500 loan and $200 "for coffee," an expression used by Yemenis for a cash gift. Mohamed went to Ohio where he had a distant relative. He had trouble finding work, and Ali, a friend of his deceased father, took him in. "Every morning Ali would cook me breakfast before he went to work and leave me $3. He took me in as his own son." When Mohamed could not find work in Ohio, Ali gave him $1,000 and a train ticket to California, where other Yemenis were employed as farmworkers. The work was difficult and the pay was little, but he was desperate. Between the years 1957–1959, he worked as a migrant worker in the fields, moving every month or six weeks. Whatever money he made would be spent traveling to his next job.

Mohamed met his Mexican American wife, Irma, in Delano, and got married in 1962. He spent all his savings, except for $30, on the wedding, including Erma's wedding dress. His Yemeni friends who attended the wedding gave him $4,000 as a wedding gift. He eventually became a supervisor at the farm where he worked, received his citizenship, and sent for his brother in Yemen. Other relatives soon followed. Mohamed and Irma have two children, both of whom are college graduates.

Hart-Cellar Act

The increase in the number of immigrants and war refugees from Lebanon, Palestine, and Iraq came shortly after the United States lifted many of its restrictive immigration laws, allowing many non-Europeans to come to the United States during the 1970s, 1980s, and 1990s.

Between 1917 and 1924 the United States passed a number of laws placing quotas and restrictions on the number of immigrants who could come from certain countries. The Immigration Act of 1924 severely limited immigration from all nations except northwestern Europe, thus limiting Arab immigration to small numbers.

In the 1960s, the Civil Rights movement succeeded in ending many racial and ethnic discriminatory laws, including immigration laws. The Immigration Act of 1965 (also known as the Hart-Cellar Act) abolished all limitations based on national origin. Arabs joined with many other people from around the world in coming to the United States to start new lives.

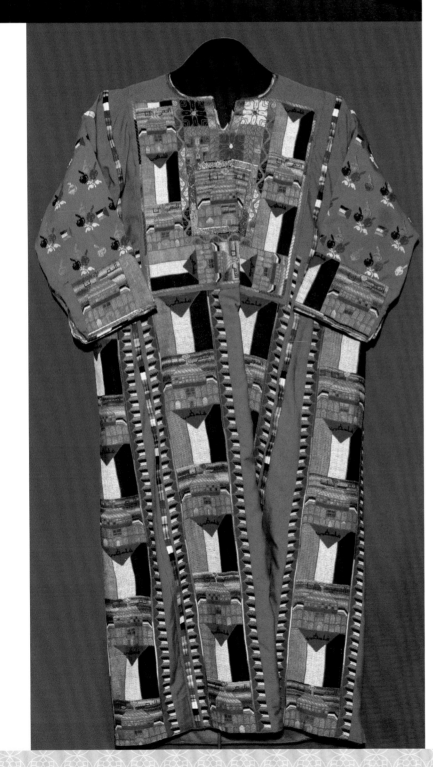

Contemporary Palestinian Dress. 1995. This embroidered dress features the flag of Palestine and the Dome of the Rock. The work of Halima Abdel Fateh.

War Refugees

Since late 1967 the majority of Arab immigrants coming to the United States have fled the horrors of war in their countries of Iraq, Lebanon, Palestine, Sudan, and Yemen.

1967 Arab-Israeli War

The Arab-Israeli War of 1967 and decades of political unrest that followed in the region contributed to the increased numbers of Arab immigration to the United States and to a heightened sense of Arab American identity. In the early part of 1967, tensions between Israel and surrounding Arab countries culminated in the Six-Day War. This war resulted in the Israeli occupation of the Palestinian territories of East Jerusalem, the West Bank, the Gaza Strip, as well as the Syrian Golan Heights, and the Egyptian Sinai Peninsula. Three-hundred thousand Palestinians became refugees; many of them subsequently settled in Jordan and several thousand immigrated to the United States.

After the Israeli occupation, **Judeh Hanna Judeh**, a tailor in Ramallah, became concerned with the safety of his family, especially his older two sons. He had already become a refugee in 1948, when he lost his home and shop in Jaffa. Along with his wife and then only child, Judeh settled in Ramallah and opened a new tailor shop. After the Israelis occupied the West Bank, Judeh decided to leave his business and start a new life in search of safety and stability for his family.

Judeh and his two sons, Hanna and Jad, left Ramallah exactly two years after the Israeli occupation. They arrived in Chicago in June 1969. He left behind his wife and seven children. A few months later, 15-year-old Jezail joined her father and two brothers.

Judeh found employment at a tailor's shop in downtown Chicago. In March 1970, his wife Victoria and five of their children joined the rest of the family. In June 1970, the whole family moved to the Detroit area. The older two sons found employment at Detroit Diesel, a car motor factory, and Judeh found a job as a tailor at Crowley's, where he worked until he retired in 1986.

Judeh Hanna Judeh and Victoria Saliba Snober, wedding photo, August 13, 1944

Judeh with his children in their apartment in Chicago

British Passport. 1939

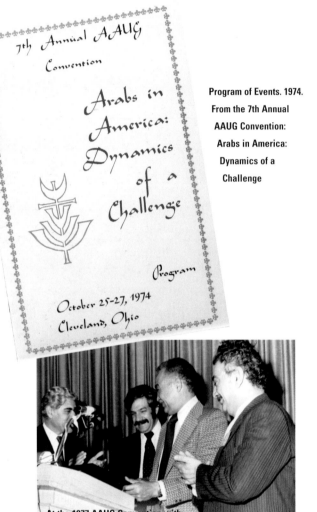

Program of Events. 1974.
From the 7th Annual
AAUG Convention:
Arabs in America:
Dynamics of a
Challenge

At the 1977 AAUG Convention with
then Detroit Mayor Coleman Young

Organizing for Political Rights

The 1967 War led to the formation of the first major Arab American national political organization, the Association of Arab American University Graduates (AAUG). Arabs in America were dismayed at the ways in which the U.S. media portrayed the war and at the U.S. government's hostility towards Arab and Arab American causes. In late 1967, a group of professionals formed the AAUG to educate the American public and policymakers about the Arab world and Arabs in the United States and to defend Arabs and Arab Americans from defamation and discrimination. The organization was similar to other minority group organizations that were forming during the time of the Civil Rights movement.

Ibrahim Abu-Lughod was an influential Palestinian scholar and activist who helped establish the AAUG. Born in 1929 in Jaffa, Palestine, Ibrahim was one of the last defenders of the city before it fell to Israeli forces in 1948. He was forced to flee and eventually moved to the United States, where he received his doctorate in Middle East Studies from Princeton University. He spent thirty-four years as a Political Science professor at Northwestern University, Illinois, where he wrote a number of books, such as *Arab Rediscovery of Europe*. In 1977, while in exile, he was elected to the Palestine National Council.

Abu-Lughod's efforts to establish a Palestinian Open University in Beirut were destroyed by the Israeli bombing of the city in 1982. He was

a lifelong voice in the struggle for Palestinian liberation, a struggle that took him back to Palestine in 1992 after forty-four years of exile. There, he taught at Bir Zeit University and worked at the Qattan Foundation, an organization that aims to advance the cultural, educational, and scientific development of Arabs and Palestinians. Upon his death in 2001, Ibrahim received his final wish to be buried in his birthplace of Jaffa.

AAUG Youth Delegation members take a break from their
t[s] of sidewalk construction

Former AAUG President
Hassan Haddad, President
Abbas Alnasrawi, and Vice
President Hani Farris meet H.
H. Sheikh Sultan Bin
Mohammed Al Qassimi in
Sharjah, U.A.E. in 1982

The Long War in Lebanon

During the early 1970s, Lebanon witnessed a series of political and economic upheavals that exploded into a seventeen-year civil war in 1975. In 1982, the Israeli Army invaded Lebanon and occupied the southern part of the country until 1997. These two major events left many parts of the country destroyed and the economy in shambles. Many Lebanese families left the country seeking a more secure life in Europe, Australia, Canada, and the United States.

The new Lebanese immigrants, especially those who came from areas that were occupied by Israel, were mostly Muslims. Many were urban, middle-class merchants and professionals. Some of the university students who were in the United States during the war found jobs and stayed. Today, in a number of cities around the world, we find concentrated Lebanese communities with a large number of recent immigrants, who often come from the same extended families and villages.

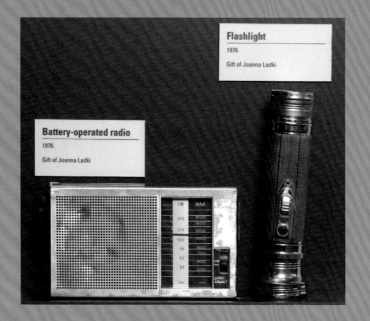

Flashlight

1976.

Gift of Joanna Ladki

Battery-operated radio

1976.

Gift of Joanna Ladki

"When we came to the United States in 1987 we brought nothing with us, just one set of clothes for each person. Before coming to the States, we were moving from one place to another as refugees. We left our village, Aitaroun, in 1978 because of the Israeli invasion of South Lebanon....When we left it we took nothing with us, we just fled for our lives. Because of the Lebanese Civil War and the Israeli occupation, we just kept moving from one place to another seeking safety. When the bombing would start, usually at night, we would run to a shelter, if there was one....We would grab our blankets, pillows, radio, and a flashlight and just run....When I was ten years old, we stayed in one shelter for a whole month....We lived on boiled potatoes. That is why when we came to America, like other Lebanese immigrants of the time, we came with nothing..." **— Nissrine Hussein**

Seeking Higher Education

Linda Jaber was one of the many Lebanese who eventually came to the United States, displaced by the political unrest in the region during the 1970s and 1980s. The Lebanese Civil War began in June of 1975. When her family returned from their annual summer vacation in South Lebanon, they found that their house in Beirut had been occupied and the family's belongings were taken or stolen. They spent the next two years at their summer home in the South until the Israeli army bombed the village market. The Jaber family then put all of their belongings into a truck and headed to another village, where they found shelter. In 1979, Linda came to the United States seeking higher education and security. She first stayed with her step-sister in Michigan and attended Wayne State University, where she graduated with a doctoral degree in Pharmacy and became a professor. Her research focuses on diabetes, especially among Arab Americans. In 1988, Linda's mother and sister came to live with her in Dearborn.

From left: Linda Jaber as a child with her family

With friends in Lebanon before leaving for the U.S. in 1979

Linda's graduation photo

Hardship in Iraq

Like the Lebanese that preceded them, Iraqis began fleeing their country in large numbers during the 1990s due to continued economic and political hardships in their country. These included the heavy human and economic cost of the ten-year war between Iraq and Iran in the 1980s, the 1991 Gulf War, the twelve years of economic sanctions that followed, and the repressive regime of Saddam Hussein.

Before the 1990s, the number of Iraqi immigrants was relatively low, with the exception of the Chaldeans, Aramaic-speaking Christians from northern Iraq.

Many Iraqis had enjoyed a high standard of living in oil-rich Iraq. Some students who had come to the United States in the 1950s ended up staying. Intellectuals and highly educated Iraqis also immigrated to the United States prior to the 1990s.

After the 1991 Gulf War, tens of thousands fled Iraq; some of them went to refugee camps in Saudi Arabia and were eventually granted refugee status and came to the United States. Many came to the Detroit area because of its large Arab American community.

The Aljaberi family

Majid in refugee camp in Saudi Arabia

Building a New Life

Layla Aljaberi and her children were among the thousands who fled Iraq after the 1991 Gulf War. When the war started, the family left their home in Baghdad and took refuge in a small village. Two months later, after the end of the war, they returned to their home. Meanwhile, Layla's son, Khaldoon, who was serving in the Iraqi Army, went missing, and eventually surrendered to American forces.

When Saddam Hussein's Baath Party came to Layla's house looking for Khaldoon, Layla became fearful for her children and decided to leave Iraq with her sons Majid, Rafid, Samer, and her daughter Faten.

Taking only some cash and clothing, the family fled to Saudi Arabia, where they lived in refugee camps for twenty months. Eventually, she found her son Khaldoon, who had been placed in a different camp. At the time, they believed that the United States would overthrow Saddam Hussein, and soon they would be able to return to their country. However, Hussein

remained in power, and the family made plans to immigrate to the United States. In 1992, they received refugee status and were able to come with five hundred other Iraqi families. By this point, they had run out of all their money. In the United States, Layla and her children were settled in Phoenix, Arizona by the Catholic Relief Agency and were given a small one-bedroom apartment. After a year, the family came to Detroit because of its large Arab American community. Khaldoon became a computer field engineer and Majid worked as a family doctor. Rafid and Faten studied to be dentists. The family eventually moved back to Phoenix, Arizona.

Majid becomes Mitch

Layla's son, **Majid**, a medical doctor, put his expertise to good use throughout the time of the family's ordeal. He graduated from medical school in Baghdad before the Gulf War. When he and his family fled to the refugee

camps in Saudi Arabia, he found them to have poor sanitation and lacking in medical care. He watched people die of minor illnesses, prompting him and other refugee doctors to organize clinics.

Later, Majid attempted to return to Iraq through a long trek across the desert. When he arrived, he found his family property confiscated and their home robbed. He was soon arrested. The government released him on the condition that he would never leave the country again; otherwise, his remaining relatives in Iraq would be punished. He managed to escape and ended up in Jordan, where he worked in a hospital until he was granted political asylum in the Netherlands. In 1994, he was finally reunited with his family in the United States. At first, he had difficulty finding work as a doctor. Upon the advice of friends, Majid changed his name to Mitch Freeman and soon after found a job as a family doctor in Arizona.

Khammi Abraham Abbo, the adult on the far right, immigrated to the United States in 1965. Taken in Telkaif, Iraq, this picture also includes her mother, Warina, and four children: Hyatt, Nazhat, Maeriam, and Youssif

John Paul Mousaly pocket watch,
he brought it with him from Syria
when he came in 1910

John Paul Mousaly, his wife and children

Chaldean Immigration

Chaldeans are Aramaic-speaking Catholic Christians who trace their origins to the ancient inhabitants of Mesopotamia (present-day Iraq).

Some Chaldeans immigrated to America as early as 1910. They followed in the footsteps of the Syrians and Lebanese and opened retail stores in cities such as Detroit and San Diego. In fact, the first Chaldean immigrants in San Diego were Jesuit-trained Chaldeans who were recruited to teach Arabic at the U.S. army base there.

With the relaxation of the quota system in the 1960s, more Chaldeans immigrated to the United States. Word of their successes traveled to Iraq and encouraged others to follow. The Iran-Iraq War of the 1980s and the 1991 Gulf War further motivated Chaldeans to leave.

Zia Al-Kas Abbo immigrated to the United States in 1923
and settled in Detroit, Michigan

John Paul Mousaly came to the United States in 1910 from Damascus, Syria. His father was originally from Mousel, Iraq, and John is believed to be one of the earliest Chaldeans to immigrate to the U.S. He initially settled in Rhode Island and later moved to Boston in 1915, where he opened a grocery store.

Asmaa Oraha Jamil immigrated to the United States from Telkaif, Iraq in 1977. Her father, Oraha Hermiz Jamil, came to the United States with three of his children, sponsored by his eldest daughter. After a short time he sent for his wife and remaining children.

Like many Chaldean families, the Jamils and his children worked in retail. Once each of his children reached the age of 16, the legal age to sell liquor, cigarettes, and lottery tickets, they began working in family-owned party store. Eventually, Asmaa's family purchased the party store business from her brother-in-law's brother. At twenty-five, already an accomplished entrepreneur, Asmaa decided to go to college, where she received a Bachelor's degree and a Master's of Business Administration.

The Jamil family in Telkaif, Iraq. Asmaa
is in the front row, second from the right

Beginning Communities

Sudan and Somalia

Immigration from Sudan and Somalia to the United States paralleled immigration from other Arab countries. Between the 1950s and 1980s, few came as students. In the 1990s, the numbers increased dramatically, as many of them were war refugees.

However, the very first documented Sudanese, Sati Majid, came as early as 1904. He became famous for converting thousands of African Americans to Islam. After Sudan achieved independence in 1956, educated Sudanese sought higher education in the United States. While most returned, some stayed. The most significant wave of immigration occurred in the 1990s, when decades of civil war reached a climax and the Sudanese faced economic and political hardships. Many immigrants sought asylum and settled in New York City and Washington, D.C.

Similarly, a small number of immigrants came from Somalia before 1965. With the relaxation of immigration laws came more immigrants. Students came to study and a few of them found jobs and stayed. But as civil war and starvation devastated Somalia in the 1990s, a larger number of refugees arrived. Today, Somali communities are emerging in midwestern cities, especially in the twin cities of Minneapolis and St. Paul in Minnesota. Others settled in large cities such as Washington, D.C., New York, and Boston.

Salma Al-Bashir was born in Sudan and has lived in various countries around the world, including England, Oman, Saudi Arabia, and Qatar. Granted political asylum, Salma arrived to the United States in 1996 with her mother and younger brother. Her father, the former High Commissioner for Refugees in the Sudan, was in New York at the time of their arrival. Her three other siblings eventually followed. Salma, and her family settled in New York City where her father worked. She lived in Brooklyn for eight years and then moved to Michigan to attend college. Salma is pursuing a career in film with the goal of dispelling stereotypes about the Arab world and Arab Americans.

Salma's family traces their roots to the Shaigia tribe in northern Sudan. It is very important for her to be able to preserve her cultural heritage and maintain her pride as an Arab, while forming her identity as an American. She hopes to travel the world and return to her native Sudan one day.

"There's no doubt that I identify myself as an African and an Arab but mostly, I think of myself as a Sudanese." — **Salma Al-Bashir**

Coming from North Africa

Historically, very few immigrants came from the North African Arab countries of Libya, Tunisia, Algeria, and Morocco. Instead, they immigrated to Europe, especially France, which colonized most of these countries. This explains why many North Africans speak French.

A few immigrants from North Africa, especially Morocco, arrived as early as the eighteenth century. But most came after the United States eased its immigration policies in 1965. Some came as students and stayed; others came as immigrants seeking better opportunities. North African immigrants are diverse in their socioeconomic backgrounds and settle in major cities such as New York, Washington, D.C., Los Angeles, and Boston.

In 1985, **Jalil Hijaouy** left Morocco in pursuit of higher education. He settled in California where he earned a Bachelor's degree in Business Administration and a Master's in English. Every two years Jalil returned to visit his family in Casablanca. On one of these trips he met Naima and they exchanged vows at a traditional wedding ceremony in1995.

Between 1998 and 1990, Jalil worked in Saudi Arabia as a university English teacher. After two years he returned to California and obtained a job as a high school teacher in Modesto. He and Naima have two children, Lina and Zakaria.

Top: Jalil, with uncle Ahmad, on a San Francisco cable car
Right: Jalil and Naima's wedding, 1995

Saudi Arabia and the Gulf

Very few people have immigrated to the United States from the Arab countries of Saudi Arabia and the Gulf States: Bahrain, Kuwait, Oman, Qatar, and the United Arab Emirates. These countries enjoy a relatively higher standard of living and offer better job opportunities than the rest of the Arab world.

For many years, people from these countries have been coming to the United States to do business, seek medical treatment, and enjoy vacations, but they rarely stayed. Students from Saudi Arabia and the Gulf States have been coming here in relatively large numbers since the 1950s. They study a variety of fields at different universities around the country. Upon graduation, the majority of these students return to their countries, where they can easily find good employment and decent living standards.

Saleh Fawaz and Zamil Al-Mikrin, students from Saudi Arabia, in Detroit, circa 1978

Arab American Settlement Map

Although Arab Americans can be found in every state of the Union, the majority of them live in large metropolitan areas such as Los Angeles, San Francisco, Detroit, Chicago, and New York City. The states with large concentrations of Arab Americans are California, Michigan, New York, Illinois, Florida, Ohio, Pennsylvania, and Texas, and the District of Columbia.

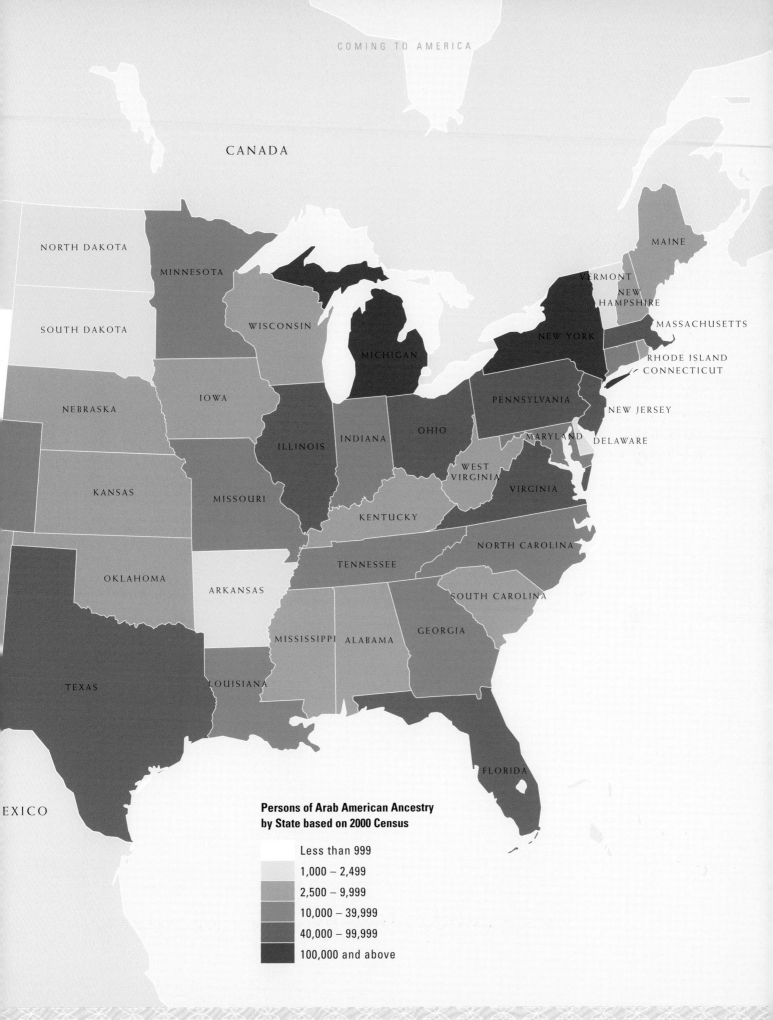

CANADA

NORTH DAKOTA

MINNESOTA

SOUTH DAKOTA

WISCONSIN

MICHIGAN

MAINE

VERMONT

NEW HAMPSHIRE

MASSACHUSETTS

NEW YORK

RHODE ISLAND

CONNECTICUT

NEBRASKA

IOWA

ILLINOIS

INDIANA

OHIO

PENNSYLVANIA

NEW JERSEY

MARYLAND

DELAWARE

KANSAS

MISSOURI

WEST VIRGINIA

VIRGINIA

KENTUCKY

NORTH CAROLINA

OKLAHOMA

ARKANSAS

TENNESSEE

SOUTH CAROLINA

GEORGIA

TEXAS

MISSISSIPPI

ALABAMA

LOUISIANA

FLORIDA

EXICO

**Persons of Arab American Ancestry
by State based on 2000 Census**

Less than 999

1,000 – 2,499

2,500 – 9,999

10,000 – 39,999

40,000 – 99,999

100,000 and above

9/11/2001

The Arab American community suffered twofold as a result of the tragic events of September 11, 2001. As all Americans, they shared the feelings of horror and grief that resulted from the attacks. They also suffered the unjust treatment of being held responsible for 9/11, although not a single Arab American was found guilty or connected to the attacks.

As of 2004, approximately two thousand Arab and non-Arab Muslim men in the United States were held as "Special Interest Detainees" without ever being charged with a crime. Later, a government investigation ruled that the basic legal rights of these detainees had been denied.

While the government placed stricter legal controls on many aspects of immigration following September 11th, special programs were adopted for persons from Arab and Muslim countries. People from these countries were subject to a new system of registration and many were deported for minor visa violations or petty offenses, which previously had been overlooked.

Coming to America became increasingly difficult for Arabs, as security checks took much longer and many were denied visas for undisclosed reasons. These new checks and regulations resulted in a substantial decrease in the number of Arabs coming as visitors and students. It is likely that the number of Arab immigrants will also decline.

After September 11, 2001, the State Department sought to question about 5000 Arab men ages 18-33, who entered the U.S. after January 2000 on tourist, immigration, business, or student visas.

Arab American community leaders in Michigan requested a meeting with the U.S. Attorney and FBI offices in Michigan. As a result this letter was sent to 700 Arab men in Michigan who were part of the sought after 5000 individuals.

In Michigan, the interviews took place without coercion. In many other states, notably New York, New Jersey and California, the men were often confronted without notice and taken from their homes, jobs or schools to be questioned.

Out of the 5000, not even one person was found to have any relation or knowledge about the events of September 11.

U.S. Department of Justice

United States Attorney
Eastern District of Michigan

---

211 W. Fort Street
Suite 2000
Detroit, Michigan 48226

AUSA Robert Cares
Telephone: (313)226-9736
Facsimile: (313)226-2372

November 26, 2001

Dearborn, MI 48126

Dear

    As you know, law enforcement officers and federal agents have been acquiring information that may be helpful in determining the persons responsible for the September 11th attacks on the World Trade Center and the Pentagon. Furthermore, they are pursuing all leads that may assist in preventing any further attacks. I am asking that you assist us in this important investigation.

    Your name was brought to our attention because, among other things, you came to Michigan on a visa from a country where there are groups that support, advocate, or finance international terrorism. **We have no reason to believe that you are, in any way, associated with terrorist activities.** Nevertheless, you may know something that could be helpful in our efforts. In fact, it is quite possible that you have information that may seem irrelevant to you but which may help us piece together this puzzle.

    Please contact my office to set p an interview at a location, date, and time that is convenient for you. During this interview, you will be asked questions that could reasonably assist in the efforts to learn about those who support, commit, or associate with persons who commit terrorism.

    While this interview is voluntary, it is crucial that the investigation be broad based and thorough, and the interview is important to achieve that goal. We need to hear from you as soon as possible - **by December 4.** Please call my office at (313) 226-9665 between 9:00 a.m. and 5:00 p.m. any day, including Saturday and Sunday. We will work with you to accommodate your schedule.

    Yours truly,

JEFFREY COLLINS
United States Attorney

ROBERT P. CARES
Assistant United States Attorney

Chapter Two
Living in America

Arab Americans have been an integral part of the history of the United States since its early days. Early Arab immigrants worked as peddlers, grocery store owners, and manual laborers. They lived in large cities and small towns, and they settled in every state.

Arab Americans are remarkably diverse. They live in rural and major metropolitan areas. Some have settled in suburban communities, whereas others live in predominantly Arab American neighborhoods. Some are upper and middle class, whereas others are struggling workers with limited incomes.

Some Arab Americans are born in this country to American-born parents and grandparents and have a limited knowledge of the Arabic language; others are recent immigrants who are fluent in Arabic but speak little English. Arab Americans are also diverse in their professions. Some are doctors and lawyers; some work in factories or on farms; many prefer to have their own businesses. Some Arab American women stay home to raise their children and take care of their families, whereas others can be found in all kinds of professions.

"Your path is easier now that you are with us"

Ahlan wa Sahlan is a greeting used to welcome visitors. Ahlan wa Sahlan signs of different designs, sizes, and shapes are found in many Arab and Arab American homes. This reflection of hospitality is very important in Arab culture. Guests, even those who arrive unexpectedly, are welcomed and asked to join the family for a meal. Many hosts would be insulted if guests refuse offers of food and drink. It is also considered impolite to ask guests if they want to drink or eat. Instead, the host simply offers food and drink to the guest.

Ahlan wa sahlan is a shortened version of Ji`eta Ahlan wa Wat`ta Sahlan, which translates into "You've come upon family and stepped onto an easy plateau," meaning that your path is easier now that you are with us.

Sewing Machine, Circa 1930. Adele Shaheen immigrated to Boston, Massachusetts in 1910. As a young woman, she began work in Boston's famous garment district and bought this sewing machine from her employer. Like many immigrants at that time, Adele did "piece work" as a primary source of income, making and repairing blouses, skirts and belts.

Quilt, Circa 1965. Sewn by Matilda Awad from the remnants of cloth brought home from a garment-making factory owned by her husband Kamel Awad and son Edward Awad. Some remnants were sewn into neckties for all the men and boys in her family; the others were used in this piece.

The Living Room

The living room is central to Arab American families. The room
tends to be large in order to accommodate family members,
relatives and guests. Many Arab American living rooms tend to
have artifacts that remind them of their original home countries

It all boils down to family

For Arab immigrants, the family is the most important social and economic institution. Early immigrants worked very hard and lived frugally to send money to their relatives in their country of origin, which they often referred to as "the old country." Once financially secure, they brought their parents, brothers, sisters, brides, uncles, aunts, cousins, and relatives of their relatives, until the whole extended family, and often the entire village, were reunited in their new homeland.

Earlier immigrants helped newcomers adjust to life in America. They provided a social cushion that helped them adjust to life in a foreign country and to a culture that is very different from their own. They helped them find employment and provided them with a place to live until they could survive on their own.

The Arab American extended family continues to thrive in many cities. Relatives live together on the same street, on the same block, and sometimes in the same home. They often work and socialize together, making it easier for them to preserve the culture and traditions they hold dear.

Many Arab Americans live as nuclear families and yet maintain strong family ties as they socialize with members of their extended families, take care of their elders, and support their relatives in need.

"I would like to answer your letter dated 10/30/74…The young man as you describe him is excellent, especially if he is not older than you…Our comments is that we would like you to serve our Arab countries with your high education and your great personality, especially Palestine…I want to tell you again that you make the decision, and you will always be our precious daughter and this will be always your home." — Your loving father

Reminders of Home

Arab Americans often bring an assortment of items back from the Arab world as reminders of the homeland. Palestinian embroidery tops the list of gifts brought back. The embroidery is usually purchased as pillow cases or ornaments to be hung on walls or doors. Paintings on papyrus paper and decorative brass plates are most commonly brought from Egypt. Cedar wood ornaments from Lebanon are popular and inlaid wood from Syria is common. From North Africa and Palestine colorful clay pottery decorated with floral patterns are also found in many homes. From Yemen and Iraq, silver jewelry is a favorite.

Religion and Culture

Religious artifacts found in Arab and Arab American homes carry not only religious meanings, but also cultural ones; prayer beads, al-kharazeh al-zarqa (eye-agate amulets), wooden engravings of Koranic verses such as Mashaa' Allah (what Allah wills), or Hatha' Min Fadlli Rabee (this is from God's grace) are found in both Christian and Muslim homes. Biblical quotes engraved in wood brought from the Cedars in Lebanon or on pottery plates brought from Palestine are found in many Christian homes.

Marriage and Family

Marriages are important celebrations among Arab American families. They are considered not only a union of the bride and the groom, but also as a union of families. Parents finance the wedding, which often includes hundreds of people, and help the couple establish their first home.

Because of their diverse religious, national, and professional backgrounds, marriage practices among Arab Americans vary from one community to another. In some cases, Arab Americans choose their own spouses and inform their families of their decision. In other cases, they meet someone they like, but wait for their families'

approval before they get engaged. Sometimes, families arrange their children's marriage to someone from their original hometown or country.

Most Arab American families prefer to see their children marry someone from a similar religious and national background. For example, a Lebanese Christian family would prefer to see their son or daughter marry a Lebanese Christian. Sometimes they would like to see their children marry someone from their original village.

Some Arab Americans, however, marry outside their ethnic and religious community.

المصور جورج تكيلا

Michael Joseph Roum and Mary Ayoub

The wedding of Michael and Mary with several priests. In the center of the photo is Antiochian Orthodox Patriarch Gregarios. Michael Joseph Roum came to New York in the early 1920s. After establishing an embroidery business, he brought over his three brothers and sister. In 1924, he returned to Damascus, Syria to marry Mary Ayoub. He was about 31 years old and she was not quite 16. They came back to New York, and in 1948 the whole family moved to California.

Dearest Son Charles

Immigrants usually leave behind family members, neighbors, and friends. Maintaining contact with loved ones, which is very important to Arab Americans, takes different forms and has changed over the years. Writing letters, which once took weeks to arrive, was the most common form of communication. As transportation improved, letters would arrive within a week or ten days. When immediate communication was necessary, family members used telegrams.

With the improvement and accessibility of technology, Arab Americans began to send tape and video recordings. As the cost of long distance phone calls became more affordable, they kept in touch with family members and friends by telephone and sometimes e-mail. Telephone cards, which provide inexpensive rates, are commonly used by Arab Americans, as well as by other immigrant communities.

The extended family continues to be very important to Arab Americans; many can trace their genealogy to several generations. This family tree belongs to the Najjar (Al-Balady) family.

The Front Porch

Many Arab Americans use their front porch to socialize with family and friends. Often friends and neighbors will just drop in for a cup of coffee, or to play a game of backgammon or cards.

Backgammon

Backgammon is one of the most popular adult games in the Arab world; it is played at homes and in coffee shops. Games similar to backgammon have been played for thousands of years in all parts of the world. The most ancient ancestor of the game that has been discovered dates back some five thousand years to the ancient civilization of Sumer, which flourished in southern Mesopotamia (modern day Iraq). After excavating the ancient city of Ur, archaeologists discovered board games that strongly resemble that of today's backgammon. There is also evidence that the Egyptian Pharaohs were enjoying a similar game known as Senat. This game, which is an ancestor of the Mesopotamian version, was regularly found in tombs of Egyptian Pharaohs.

Argileh (water pipe)

The Kitchen

Kitchen and food are very important to Arab Americans. The kitchen is the place where women often get together to cook or to socialize. Food is usually prepared in large quantities, just in case relatives or neighbors stop by.

Shatila In 1979, Mr. Raid Shatila, a Lebanese immigrant, founded Shatila Food Products in Dearborn, Michigan. The Arabic bakery provides a variety of different products, including traditional baklava and tissue-thin pastry with fresh nuts and sweet syrup. Shatila bakers prepare the desserts using ingredients and methods similar to those used by artisans in the Arab world for thousands of years. Based in the Midwest, the bakery is now famously known throughout the United States and Canada for its Arabic sweets.

LIVING IN AMERICA

"This story was sprinkled in the olive oil we sprinkled on our hummus." — Suheir Hammad

Family and Food

Food is an integral element of the cultural identity. Specific foods mark important cultural and religious events. Christian Arabs, for example, fast during Lent and eat delicious meatless dishes, of which there are many in the Arab world. In many Arab American homes, the Thanksgiving turkey is accompanied by an even more essential entrée, hashweh—rice with lamb, nuts, and spices, which is either stuffed in the turkey or cooked separately.

Sweets also play a large part in Arab and Arab American social life. Special sweets are eaten on religious holidays and festive days and are distributed at celebrations of births, weddings, circumcisions, and are presented as gifts. Ka'ak b'ajweh (date-filled rings) and mamoul (dough filled with either walnuts or pistachios) are special sweets associated with both Christian and Muslim holidays. Katayef, a popular pastry filled with nuts, cream, or cheese and dipped in syrup, is especially made during the month of Ramadan.

To mark the birth of a child, special creamy puddings garnished with nuts, such as mughlee, are made for well-wishers, and the mother drinks a tea of caraway for its cleansing and restorative properties.

Certain foods, such as stuffed vegetables, grape leaves, cabbage rolls, and stews, are often prepared in large quantities and served warm to meet the culture of hospitality. Since there are always guests coming and going, it is difficult to know how many will be sharing a meal.

Cookie press
This is used in shaping and imprinting a design on mamoul, traditionally a ground walnut-filled cookie. Made especially for the Eid (Muslim holidays) and Easter, mamoul today is also filled with pistachios and dates. At Easter, these cookies are often served with date rings, another special holiday sweet.

Melody Farms Milk: Originally known as Tom George and Sons Dairy Distributors, Melody Farms began with a clientele consisting of just one route with three accounts. With sales in excess of $130 million, the company today owns and operates two processing plants and remains one of the largest privately owned dairy and beverage distribution companies in the United States.

Famous Chili: Around the turn of the century, Mama Joe and Papa Joe Korkmas came to the United States from Lebanon, eventually settling in Fort Smith, Arkansas, where they opened "The Famous Café." Their chili became so popular that Papa Joe began packaging it in one-pound hand-wrapped bricks to sell to his customers at the café. He then decided to market the chili for retail sales in grocery stores around the state. Sales were so high that he established the Famous Chili Company in 1935. Today, the company is still owned and operated by the Korkmas family, now in its third generation. Famous Brand Chili is still made using the time-tested recipe that Papa Joe used to start the company over 60 years ago.

Soup tureen and matching bowls. 2003.
Representative of North African pottery, such
sets are often used throughout Ramadan

"None was more important than

the others…all were guests."

— D.H. Melham

The Teen's Room

Like other youngsters, Arab Americans are faced with issues that are common to teenagers in America. However, Arab American teenagers are often faced with additional pressure from their parents who want them to maintain their Arab cultural heritage.

Writing Arabic

Some Arab Americans born in the United States do not speak Arabic; others speak Arabic with their parents and grandparents, but they do not know how to write in Arabic. Because language is an important aspect of cultural identity, many young Arab Americans who were born in the United States, or immigrated at an early age, chose to learn Arabic at college or in summer language programs.

The Arabic language has two forms, fussha, or classical Arabic, and a'mmeya, colloquial Arabic. A'mmeya has regional dialects; for example, someone from Morocco speaks Arabic differently than someone from Lebanon. Fussha, a more official form, is understood by people across the Arab world. Both spoken and written, fussha is used in news broadcasts and in the newspapers.

Button. 1993.

Patch. 2003.
In celebration of
Fordson High School's
75th anniversary

Fordson Football Team

Fordson High School, built in 1928, serves as a historic landmark in the city of Dearborn, Michigan. Fordson's head football coach Jeff Stergalas says that during his 23-year tenure the makeup of the student body has changed. Once heavily Greek and Italian, today Fordson's student population is roughly 92% Arab American.

Fordson's football team, the Tractors, is known for its strong program. In 1993, the Tractors won the Michigan State Championship. Like other high school football teams, the Tractors have to balance academics, family, and football. In 2003, the team was working hard to continue the school's winning tradition, when faced with another challenge—fasting for the Muslim holy month of Ramadan while striving towards the state championship. Fasting means abstaining from food and drink during daylight hours. Ramadan, the ninth month in the lunar calendar, occurs approximately eleven days earlier each year. In 2003, Ramadan began in October and extended into November. This faith-based practice heavily affected the 2003-04 Tractor team, since all but two players were Muslim.

Head Coach Stergalas worked hard to accommodate his players. He made sure there was no water on the field during practice and held some practices at night to ease stress on players. Most importantly, teammates took time out during practice to break the fast together at sunset. One Tractor player commented that fasting did what it was supposed to do; it gave him a sense of inner strength.

"Seek knowledge from the crib to the grave"

Education and learning are highly valued among Arab Americans. This is due in part to the tradition of scholarship in the Arab world among scientists and others. For example, the world's first educational institutions and hospitals were established in the Arab world. There are many Arabic proverbs that reflect the importance of education, such as "pursue knowledge all the way to China," "childhood education is like etching in stone," and "seek knowledge from the crib to the grave." Teaching is a highly valued profession, and educators are given much respect in Arab society. A famous Arabic saying highlights this ethic: "Thy who teaches me one letter, I owe them for the rest of my life."

Growing Up Activist

Faced with the normal issues of teenage life in America paired with the pressure to maintain Arab cultural norms, many Arab Americans were raised in two overlapping worlds. Many values common in the larger American society, such as individualism and independence, conflict with the general values of Arab culture that emphasize collectivity and interdependence. However, many Arab Americans, proud of their Arab heritage and their identity as Americans, are able to bridge the two cultures. Many second- and third- generation Arab Americans are reclaiming their Arab heritage. Their activism is reflected in the arts, literature, film, and politics, and in many local and national organizations that have been created to address the needs and concerns of all Arab Americans.

"Arab American Youth Working for Achievement"

On Saturday February 28, 2004, ACCESS-Ohio held its first annual youth leadership conference. The theme of the conference was "Arab American Youth Working for Achievement," bringing together youth and a number of community leaders such as the Honorable Mayor Jane Campbell and ACCESS-Ohio Director Mahmoud Awadallah. Held over two days, the conference provided a forum for workshops on building leadership skills, conflict resolution, and community involvement. The event also included inspiring performances by Iron Sheik, an Arab American rap artist, and the nationally recognized artist and cartoonist Khalil Bendib. With the goal of involving Arab American youth in their communities, the Youth Leadership Conference succeeded in demonstrating the energy and activism among Ohio's Arab American community.

The Americorps volunteers who planned the conference with their director, Mahmoud and his wife, Linda

"...the same rights we had been yearning for..."

The Martin Luther King, Jr. celebration is one of the American-Arab Anti-Discrimination Committee's (ADC) largest projects in Michigan. It is an essay contest in which Arab American high school students write essays relating their own experience to Dr. King's lifetime goal of fighting for civil rights and equality for all Americans. The winning essay writers receive scholarships to the college they plan to attend.

In 2003 Layla Almaliky won first prize. Here are excerpts of her essay:

"I was six years old when the gulf war broke out in 1991.... Hell raged its bitterness on the land of Mesopotamia and demolished its peace.... Black rain fell from the sky...we managed to escape to Saudi Arabia...we lived in the desert in poor conditions for five years. Then, one day we were selected to be taken as refugees to America.... In school I learned about Dr. Martin Luther King.... It made me very proud to learn that a black man in America had been fighting for the same rights we had been yearning for under the bombshells and rockets that were raining over our heads in Iraq.

He [King] fought, struggled, and died for the sake of freedom. He shared his dreams with millions of believers around the world.... I deeply believe that one day with joined efforts of all of us, Americans, united with our legendary humanitarian causes that our ancestors shed blood for; we will live the dream of the great Martin Luther King."

Nick Hawatmeh

At eight years old, Jordanian American Nick Hawateh asked his father to drive him to the Republican headquarters so he could volunteer with the Republican Party. Since then, Nick's love of politics has grown. He has worked on numerous campaigns, such as Leslie Touma for Congress and Spencer Abraham for Senate. In 2004, 20-year-old Nick ran for Macomb County Commissioner. When he was a student at Wayne State University, Nick used to speak at local high schools, encouraging students to register to vote.

"I was born and raised in the United States. When I was 16, I went to Yemen with my parents. We went there because my sister was getting married.

I was shocked at how different I was from my people in Yemen. Although I am an American, my parents raised me and my siblings, the way they were raised back in Yemen. They strongly held on to our traditions. Yemen's newer generation seemed to have more modern ideas than us. The women I met were very open, they wanted to finish their education, go to college, work, and eventually get married, while my American sister was getting married before obtaining her high school diploma.

At first, I felt culture shocked. I was feeling like I don't belong here nor did I belong there. In Yemen, people treated me as a tourist and I found it hard to relate to or communicate with women my age. For most Americans, their first impression of me is that I may be a new immigrant, because I look ethnic. So in the past I felt that I had to prove myself constantly, at school as well as at my jobs. After maturing, I learned the differences more and accepted them. Today, I find myself comfortable knowing I have the best of both the worlds." — Anissa

"Skate or Die!"

Tajrid (Taji) Ameen was born in New York City in 1989. His father is a well-known jazz drummer, and his mother has a career working in various museums and art institutions. Taji's first love is definitely skateboarding, which he began when he was seven years old.

Over the years, Taji has appeared in many magazines, several skateboard videos, and is sponsored by different skateboard and skateboard-related companies, including Zoo York, Supreme, and Etnies. His specialty is "street-style" skating, which considers peer recognition to be most important; people skate for the sheer love of it, as expressed in the well know dictum "Skate or die!" In fact, skateboarding almost has a certain Zen-like quality to it; for it is truly about the discipline and dedication, not frustration; how else would we explain the willingness to practice a single trick for hours on end only to get it right once and then do it all over again the next day? Although skateboarding is not a team sport, it is only through sharing and securing the approval of your fellow skaters does the sport gain its credibility and ultimate advancement. A talented flutist, Taji performed at Carnegie Hall in 2003 with the Manhattan Boroughwide Orchestra. He has appeared in numerous magazines and TV commercials. Taji plans to pursue a career in the skateboarding industry.

Skateboard
Circa 2003.

Arab Americans and Religion

Early Arab immigrants were mostly Christians, with a smaller number of Muslims. Although Muslim Arabs started to arrive in larger numbers after 1965, the majority of Arab Americans continue to be Christians. Some Arab Jews came to the United States from Arab countries such as Yemen, Iraq, Morocco, and Syria.

The 1951 Ordination of Bishop Shaheen, Indianapolis, Indiana

Imam Mohamed Jawad Chirri came to the United States in 1949. Originally from Lebanon, he founded the Islamic Center of Detroit (later, the Islamic Center of America) in 1963.

The wedding of Maheda and Manuel Najjar, Chaldean Americans who immigrated to the United States in 1963

A Faithful Servant: Reverend Thomas Skaff

The Very Reverend Thomas Skaff is the first American born of Arab heritage to be ordained to the priesthood in this country. He was ordained by the Metropolitan Archbishop Antony Bashir on his name day, October 6, 1946, in his hometown of Sioux City, Iowa. He belonged to a generation of clergy pioneers who were able to bridge between earlier priests who were born or ordained in the "old country" and those who formally studied in Orthodox seminaries in the United States.

Reverend Skaff studied with a priest serving the small Iron Mountain, Michigan parish of St. Mary Antiochian Orthodox Church. He and his wife Elaine Khoury served eight parishes.

The sixth of twelve children, Rev. Skaff was born in Sioux City, Iowa in 1915 to Joseph and Sadie Ghosn Skaff, both Lebanese immigrants from the village of Ain Arab.

A humble, hospitable, and compassionate man, Rev. Skaff was deeply devoted to his faith, family, and Arab heritage. He married Elaine Khoury in Iron Mountain on August 25, 1946 and they had four children. The Skaff family members were active community members who participated in religious, social, and civic events. They warmly embraced their entire community. Reverend Skaff was a strong advocate of the Palestinian cause and was frequently hosted by local radio and television stations.

Skaff guided the building of two Texas churches, cofounded the Orthodox Clergy Association of Southwest Texas, and was serving a mission parish in Houston at the time of his death in June 1989.

Arab American Muslims

The few thousand Arab Muslims, including Sunni, Shi'a, and Druze, who came during the Great Migration era of 1880–1920, were scattered throughout the United States. The first mosque in America was not built until the early twentieth century. Before this, most Muslims met and worshipped in private homes. By the early 1920s, three mosques were built in Highland Park, Michigan (1919), Cedar Rapids, Iowa (1920), and Michigan City, Indiana (1925).

Unlike mosques in the Arab world, which serve primarily religious functions, mosques in the United States acquired social and cultural significance as Arab Muslims struggled to maintain their Arab and Muslim identity and culture.

Most Arab Americans belong to one of the two main branches of Islam—Sunni or Shi'a—a division that occurred shortly after the death of the Prophet Muhammad. Some are Druze, which is another denomination of Islam, found mostly in Lebanon, Syria, and Palestine.

Muslim Significant Dates and Holidays

Ramadan: The ninth month of the lunar calendar and considered to be the holiest month in Islam. Muslims abstain from food and drink from sunrise to sunset. This holy month symbolizes when Prophet Muhammad began receiving his first revelations from God.

Ashura: A somber religious occasion that comes on the tenth day of the lunar month of Muharram. It commemorates a ten-day mourning period for the death of Prophet Muhammad's grandson, Hussein, who Shi'a Muslims believe was the rightful leader of the Muslim people after the Prophet.

Muslim holidays follow the lunar calendar, which has 354 days—eleven days less than the 365-day Gregorian calendar used by most of the world. Therefore, Muslim holidays fall on the same day according to the lunar calendar but occur eleven days earlier each year on the Gregorian calendar. The major Muslim holidays are:

Eid al-Fitr or Eid al-Sageer (holiday of breaking the fast or the small holiday): A three-day holiday that occurs at the end of the fasting month of Ramadan.

Eid al-Adha or Eid al-Kabeer (holiday of the sacrifice or the big holiday): A four-day holiday that observes Prophet Abraham's attempt to sacrifice his son Ismail to God and the miraculous appearance of a lamb to be sacrificed instead. The holiday marks the end of the Hajj, the annual pilgrimage to the city of Mecca. Muslims celebrate this holiday by following the tradition of sacrificing a lamb and giving it to the needy.

The Five Pillars of Islam

Shahada (Declaration of Faith): The Shahada states, "There is no God but God, and Prophet Muhammad is his messenger."

Salat (Prayer): Muslims are required to pray five times a day: at dawn, noon, mid-afternoon, sunset, and nightfall.

Soum (Fasting): During the holy month of Ramadan, Muslims are required to refrain from food and drink during daylight hours. Exceptions are made for the elderly, young children, the ill, those traveling, and pregnant, nursing and menstruating women.

Zakat (Charity): Muslims are required to give a minimum of 2.2 to 2.5% of their wealth to the less fortunate each year. However, charity in all forms is encouraged throughout the year.

Hajj (Pilgrimage): The Hajj is an annual pilgrimage to Mecca in Saudi Arabia, and every Muslim who is physically and financially able is obligated to perform the journey once in his or her lifetime.

Arab American Christians

Early Arab Christian immigrants first worshiped in private homes or in public spaces used for other purposes. Some Christians worshiped in churches close to their homes. As the communities grew and became more affluent, they built their own churches. The first churches built by Christian immigrants from the Arab world were on the East Coast. Between 1880 and 1895, three churches were built in New York: Maronite, Melkite, and Eastern Orthodox. In 1890, a Maronite church was built in Boston, Massachusetts. In Michigan, the first Arab church, also a Maronite church, was built in downtown Detroit in 1898. Today there are thousands of Arab churches in every city and major town in the United States.

Christian Significant Dates and Holidays

Lent: Christians in the Arab world observe Lent for forty days before Easter by abstaining from meat, eggs, and dairy products. Elaborate vegetarian meals, referred to as Siami, are cooked during this period. Now, many Arab Americans, especially the young, observe Lent by giving up only one food item that they really enjoy, such as soda or chocolate. During this time, Arab American churches hold special masses every Wednesday evening, in which chanting (taraneem) in a distinctive eastern style is performed as the main part of prayer.

Christmas: Christmas is a special time for the extended family to get together, have elaborate meals, observe mass at midnight, and exchange gifts. Although many Christians in the Arab world celebrate Christmas on January 7th, the majority of Arab Americans celebrate Christmas on December 25th. The Egyptian Coptic Church, however, continues to celebrate Christmas on January 7th.

The tradition of gift giving is mostly limited to children, though adults may give their elderly parents simple gifts. In the United States, exchanging numerous and expensive gifts has become a very important component of Christmas for Arab American Christians and even for some Muslims.

Rogations of Nineveh: Three weeks before Lent, Chaldean and Assyrian Americans (Catholics from Iraq and Syria) fast for three days from midnight to midday, abstaining from meat and dairy products. The Rogations of Nineveh commemorate the time when it is believed that God sent the Prophet Jonas to the people of Nineveh to warn them to repent in order to avoid the destruction of their city.

Palm Sunday: Palm Sunday is the Sunday before Easter. It commemorates the entrance of Jesus Christ to Jerusalem before his death. In Jerusalem, Palestinian Christians observe this day by reenacting the entry of Jesus Christ to their city. Arab American Christians celebrate this holiday by attending special church services. Children wear new clothes bought especially for the occasion and enter the church carrying palm branches decorated with flowers and colorful ribbons with candles of all shapes and sizes.

Easter: Among Arab Christians, Easter, which honors the day when Jesus rose from the dead, is the most important Christian holiday. The two days before Easter are called Al-Juma' Al-Hazeena (Sad Friday, the Friday Jesus was crucified) and Sabt Al-Noor (Bright Saturday). Easter day is called Ahad Al-Suroor (Happy Sunday). On this day the traditional "good morning" greeting is replaced with "Christ has risen."

Saint Barbara's Holiday: Many Arab Americans observe December 4, the day that marks the death of a Christian saint named Barbara. The day is observed simply by cooking a special dish called Burrbara, which is made of wheat grain, sugar, cinnamon, a variety of nuts, and raisins.

Holy water from the Jordan River.

Work

American Pioneers:
Homesteading in North Dakota

Arab American Pioneers: Homesteading in North Dakota

Between 1890 and World War I, hundreds of courageous Syrians and Lebanese came to North Dakota to homestead. A smaller number came during the 1920s and '30s. These pioneers were both Muslim and Christian and some were women. The descendents of these pioneers still reside in North Dakota, and with their population in the thousands, they constitute an important segment of North Dakota's current population.

In 1897, the first Syrians homesteaded in Shepherd Township. That same year, more settled in Pierce County. In 1901, a post office named "Beyrout" was established in a Syrian enclave of Pierce County. Attas David ran the post office until 1906.

The U.S. Homestead Act made it possible for many poor people, including new immigrants, to own farmland.

Any U.S. citizen, or individual with the intention of becoming a citizen, who was at least twenty-one years old, could apply to homestead. In exchange for a 160-acre land deed, the U.S. Government required a five-year residency and cultivation of a large part of the land. The Homestead Act appealed to many immigrants, as they were not required to speak English or provide cash up front.

Although providing a relatively easy means of acquiring land, homesteading was difficult. Homestead laws required individuals to reside on the land, which meant living miles from other individuals and hundreds of miles from town. The severe winters of North Dakota increased the sense of isolation and many homesteaders left before the end of their five-year residency.

Bible
Circa 1905. This bible belonged to Joseph and Lamore Owan Kellel, who settled in Sheridan County, North Dakota in 1903.

Walking Across America

In the late 1800s and early 1900s, peddling was a common profession among Arab Americans. Peddling was attractive to early immigrants because it required neither savings nor proficiency in English and yielded relatively high income. As Arab peddlers sold household goods door-to-door in small and rural areas not well served by stores, they settled in these areas and opened stores. A whole industry arose out of peddling in which Arab suppliers stationed themselves in certain towns along the peddling routes that served as supply stations and resting points.

Before the end of the nineteenth century there were several successful Syrian manufacturers, importers, and wholesalers in New York City. Trade in oriental rugs and linens also flourished. The Syrians imported goods from China, the Philippines, Syria, Italy, and France. They also employed individuals to make lace and embroidery in their own homes. They would then sell the goods to peddlers as far as Texas and California.

Peddlers became such a recognizable feature of the American landscape, that one of the main characters of the famous musical *Oklahoma!* is a peddler.

Zina Essa was one of the earliest female peddlers. After coming to America alone, she worked as a peddler in order to pay for her family's passage to the United States from Lebanon. When her family arrived, she settled and lived with them in Flint, Michigan.

After immigrating from Lebanon in 1906, **M.K. Massad** settled in Oklahoma and began peddling linens and other items to rural communities in Oklahoma and Northern Texas. He used this trunk to move items to small towns and from farm to farm.

Elias Saleh immigrated to the United States in 1895 at the age of 16. Shortly after his arrival, he began peddling throughout the American Southwest. His big trade item was pocket watches. Elias settled in Detroit, Michigan, where he became a wholesaler for other peddlers, eventually opening grocery stores throughout the area in an effort to establish other family members in business.

Three generations of working women

(1879–1966)

Marwa Nader

Born in the village of Abdelli in Lebanon, Marwa Nader could neither read nor write, but throughout her life she lived in Lebanon, Europe, South America, and the United

"I didn't know what he was saying. . ."

States. In each country she learned the language "on the job."

World War I caused much economic strife in Marwa's village in Lebanon. Some of the people in her village, who had loaned Marwa's husband money, became frustrated and held Marwa responsible for the debts her husband had accumulated before immigrating to the United States. She sold her jewelry and with her daughters, Azzizy and Elizabeth, left Lebanon for Marseilles. After two years, she had saved enough money to travel to New York. In 1921, Marwa and her daughters arrived at Ellis Island.

(1914–2002)

Elizabeth Joan AbiNader

When the train arrived in Uniontown, Pennsylvania, Elizabeth's mother dropped to her knees and kissed the floor. A man approached them and her mother hugged him. Seeing her father for the first time was a shock for the seven-year-old Elizabeth.

Her father owned a gas station and general goods store, where Elizabeth and her sister worked. She loved school, but by the time she was sixteen she was driving the family peddling truck most of the week.

In 1935, Elizabeth returned to Lebanon and married her first cousin. The couple immigrated to the United States a year later.

While her husband peddled to the coal miners in Masontown, Pennsylvania, Elizabeth managed their store. She was

"Nothing about my life went as planned"

active in the community, and together the couple had six children. In 1965, the family moved to Carmichaels, Pennsylvania, where Elizabeth became the major buyer and supervisor of the family store.

(1954–)

Elmaz Abinader

The three elements of growing up with Jean and Elizabeth Abinader were poetry, prayer, and song. Elmaz's home was filled with voices, both in Arabic and English, and sometimes in the Portuguese her father had learned in Brazil.

Elmaz followed her parents' passions. A poet, author, and performer, Elmaz—like her five brothers and sisters—pursued

"A kind of bravery I couldn't imagine"

advanced degrees, completing her Ph.D. in 1985. She became a professor of creative writing at Mills College. She travels throughout the world to read and perform her work.

Her family story was the first inspiration for her work. When her father unearthed some family diaries, she realized that the voices of the women were missing. Elmaz interviewed as many women in her family as possible to acquire the female perspective on the family history.

Her play, *Country of Origin*, is about three generations of women in her family.

"When they called me to the table, I put my passport on the table and stood completely still. The clerk read my name in a way I never heard before. He looked at the passport picture of me and my two daughters. I was wearing the same polka-dotted dress that day in the inspection room as I had worn for the photograph. I didn't know what he was saying. I stood quietly until he stamped my papers and let me through.

We left on our journey to find their father."

Generations at Work

Ownership of grocery stores has its roots in peddling, in which Arab immigrants who saved money stationed themselves at certain points along peddling routes to re-supply other peddlers. Some had resting homes where peddlers could rest for a few days, buy more supplies, and continue on their journey. Gradually, more peddlers were able to save money, give up the road, and open their own produce stand or a grocery store. Once an immigrant opened a store, he or she would send for family members to come to the United States and work in the family store. Some immigrants landed along the Mexican-U.S. border and opened specialty stores catering to Mexicans. In the Southwest, Arab Americans opened stores that sold Native American jewelry.

While the children of earlier immigrants moved out of store ownership and into other areas of employment, new immigrants have been taking over the stores and retail businesses. This is made possible due to credit and loan support from earlier immigrants to newer ones. Many Arab American family members are willing to pool their resources and work together. It is not unusual to find a family of three generations working together in one family business.

Ameen Farah

Originally from Palestine, members of the Farah family were peddlers by trade. Some of the earliest immigrants in Flint, Michigan, the family established one of the first retail grocery chains in their city.

Born in Nazareth in 1889, Ameen Farah escaped to Egypt after being drafted by the Ottoman army. In 1913, he immigrated to the United States and spent most of his life in Flint. He joined the U.S. army and secured citizenship for himself and his wife. Throughout his life, he was involved in several business ventures, from rugs to wholesale food. Active in the community, Ameen helped establish Saint George Orthodox Church and the Arab American Social Center in Pleasant Lake. He died in 1975 and is buried at Grace Lawn Cemetery.

Between 1912 and 1929, the Farah family partnered with the Khoury family to establish the Farah-Khoury grocery chain, which operated nineteen stores in the Flint area. Much of the profits went to financing friends and relatives who were trying to start their own businesses. Ameen also created the A. Farah and Co. Wholesale Food Warehouse. In operation until 1929, the warehouse was destroyed due to a fire. The company was then purchased by Sam Farah, Ameen's brother-in-law, and became the Central Wholesale Company.

Within a Farah-Khouri market. Anton Gantos stands behind the counter, Ameen Farah is leaning on the counter

"The Most of the Best for the Least"

In 1911, cousins Kamol and Michael Hamady founded the Hamady Brothers' Grocery in Flint, Michigan. The business flourished and the cousins established the Hamady Brothers' Grocery chain. At one point, the chain boasted thirty-nine stores, dominating the Flint area and employing up to thirteen hundred people. The Hamady markets were the first stores of their time to let a customer shop on their own without the help of a clerk to retrieve groceries. Members of the Hamady family operated the stores for over sixty years.

A "showcase store," opened in 1940, demonstrated innovative touches with automatic doors and refrigerator cases that allowed customers to help themselves. The showcase store contained custom ceramic wall tiles, mirrored pillars, terrazzo floors, and light yellow exterior brick. Right: The Grand Opening of a Hamady Bros. Store. Fireworks, bagpipe music by Flint's own Scottish Bank, and free prizes and groceries drew large crowds of customers to the store opening.

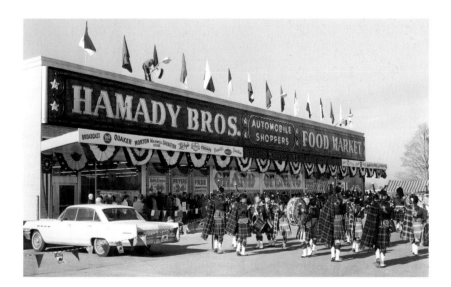

"Drive a Little and Save a Lot"

One of the early pioneers in the Flint, Michigan area, Thomas Mansour came from Palestine in 1913. He experienced much hospitality from George Saiegh, a grocery store owner who taught him the trade of butchering. In 1929, Thomas opened Citizens Market, where shoppers found all of their grocery needs under one roof. He rented out space to various vendors, enabling shoppers to buy meats, baked goods, flowers, candies, and dairy products in one store. During the Great Depression, he acquired sole ownership of the store and was able to install centralized check-out areas. Thomas's novel idea is considered by some to be the first modern-day grocery store!

After flooding nearly destroyed the building, Thomas moved his enterprise out to a farm he owned. After placing a four-page ad in the newspaper with the motto, "Drive Out a Little and Save a Lot," Mansour's business flourished.

Arab Americans' involvement in grocery business in Flint, Michigan is only one example of the extent to which Arab Americans have been involved in family owned and run grocery stores. This pattern can be found in many cities and towns throughout the USA.

From Farmer's Market to Grocery

In 1905, 18-year-old Nageeb K. Jamail ("Jim") left the mountainside village of Bekfaya in Lebanon to settle in Houston, Texas. In spite of his limited skills in English, Jim was in business for himself within six months of arriving to Houston, selling fruits and vegetables at the Houston Farmer's Market. He soon developed a loyal clientele that spanned over generations.

During the Great Depression, Jim and his wife Mary lost everything. Through the years, however, they succeeded in rebuilding the business. In 1946, after returning from World War II, their three sons worked with Nageeb and the produce business grew into a small grocery store, Jim Jamail & Sons. Jim's two daughters worked alongside the family and the store grew into a large grocery store. Jim died in 1957 before their new facility was built, but his legacy is carried on by his children and grandchildren.

President and Mrs. John Kennedy, President and Mrs. Lyndon Johnson, President and Mrs. George H. W. Bush, and Governor and Mrs. John Connally of Texas are some of Jim's most famous customers.

From top: Jim Jamail and his three sons in their first store. Left to right: Jim, Harry, Albert, and Joe. Center: The first Jim Jamail & Sons grocery store, 1946. Lower: Jim Jamail & Sons' 1959 facility in River Oaks, a Houston, Texas neighborhood. This store was remodeled and enlarged five times in thirty years.

1926. Original office suite from J.M. Haggar's office at the Santa Fe Building in Dallas, Texas.

Haggar: From Rags to Riches

Joseph Marion Haggar's life story is a typical "rags to riches" tale. Born in 1892 in the mountain village of Jezeen, Lebanon, Joseph left his home and headed to North America at age thirteen. Like many other Arab immigrants, he began his new life in Mexico as a penniless immigrant. There, he worked as a peddler and developed his skills as a salesman. Very soon, he became fluent in Spanish and four years later, he became fluent in English as well. Eventually he entered the United States, where he worked as a dishwasher, a cotton grader, and a salesman for a wholesale dry-goods company. He even sold overalls on the road. Twenty years after leaving Lebanon, he started his own business and soon became a household name in the men's dress slacks industry.

On January 22, 1923, J. M. Haggar, Sr. became a naturalized citizen of the United States. In 1976, he was awarded the Horatio Alger Award for his successful business achievements. At age eighty-five he was still working.

With only a few sewing machines and four full-time employees, Joseph founded the Haggar Company in 1926 in an old Santa Fe building in Dallas, Texas. He worked with his two sons, Ed and Joe Jr., to provide quality slacks for the workingman. People often claim that Joseph Haggar brought to the men's slacks industry what Henry Ford brought to the automobile industry—mass production. Haggar's assembly line started his company on a pattern of growth that would soon establish it as the world's largest manufacturer of dress slacks.

Joseph Haggar's keen eye for design and his unusual sense of style helped the Haggar Company sweep the men's dress slacks market. His company introduced wash 'n' wear slacks, finished-bottom dress slacks, and permanent-press slacks. In 1970, Haggar changed the way men dressed by introducing the double-knit slacks at popular prices. Seventy-five years after its founding, the Haggar Company became one of the world's largest apparel manufacturers.

Hannah Shakir

Hannah Shakir's life in the textile industry began when her family moved from Boston, Massachusetts to nearby Fall River.

Around 1920, Hannah and her brother Naseeb opened a small apron factory in the East Boston neighborhood where they lived. Nasseb cut the fabric, Hannah sewed, and their brother Elias drummed up customers along his sales route. Though they were initially successful, a move to downtown Boston significantly raised their costs and the business floundered. For the next twenty years, Hannah worked for others.

Shortly after World War II, when she was fifty, Hannah started a small sportswear factory. She began with half a dozen sewing machines in a suburban storefront and then expanded, hiring more stitchers, mostly neighborhood women.

Hannah never made a lot of money, but she loved her work. She could never understand people who retired before they had to do so. She retired at age 71. To her, life and work were the same. Neither was easy; both were good.

"When we moved…I didn't go to school anymore. I had to work. At first, I made about seven or eight dollars a week…. I learned how to operate the looms, six big looms, just like a man…. It was hard work. When I first started, we used to work twelve hours a day, from six in the morning 'til six at night and Saturdays 'til noon. I was fourteen years old."— Hannah Shakir

Locker Room

Arab Americans can be found in every profession imaginable. Their professions range from CEOs of major corporations, to assembly line and farm workers. Some are police officers and firefighters; while others are teachers, scientists, and lawyers. Many prefer to have their own businesses.

Tarick Salmaci, boxer
"The Arabian Prince"

Tarick Salmaci's dreams came true. Born in 1972 to Lebanese parents, Tarick began boxing at age eight at the Joe Hamoud Center in Dearborn, a recreation center designed to keep youth off the streets. At age eleven, he won his first amateur state championship and his first amateur U.S. Championship two years later. His prestigious list of amateur accomplishments include: six-time Michigan state championship, four-time Midwest Champion, three-time U.S. Champion, and Olympian trials finalist. In 1992, he went professional and became the North American Super Middleweight Champion in 1997. After rising to become the world's fourth-rated contender, Tarick retired in 2001. He often visits recreation centers to talk with youth about the benefits of staying off the streets.

g gloves

Tarick Salmaci's
al debut at the Palace of
ls on August 25th, 1992.
n the match by TKO.

ick Salmaci

"From the first day I laced up my gloves, I always wanted to be a champion. It has been my goal all my life to be champion."

— **Tarick Salmaci**

Manuel Hassien and Cheryl Hassien, police officers

As police officers in Michigan, Manuel Hassien and his daughter Cheryl make an impressive father-daughter team.

Born in Michigan, Manuel worked at McClouth Steel as a teenager until applying to the Dearborn Police Department. In 1955, he became the first Arab American reportedly to be hired by the Dearborn Police. Initially, many officers refused to be his partner, yet as time passed his personal and professional reputation helped improve the situation. Serving on the force for over 32 years, he worked as a patrolman, detective, sergeant, and lieutenant. He also led the Youth Bureau and Special Operations Divisions. In 1987, Manuel passed away, but his daughter, Cheryl Hassien followed in his footsteps.

Upon graduating from college, Cheryl planned on becoming a teacher. However, after learning that the Wayne County Sheriff's Department was hiring women, she applied and joined the force in 1980. Her most honorable year was 1995, when she worked on a collaborative six-agency initiative, which included the FBI. During her service, when asked to choose a call name, she chose "OMAR" in tribute to her father's call name, given to him by his troops.

Hussein Muflahi, steel worker

Many Arab Americans found employment in the steel industry in cities such as Birmingham, Alabama, Buffalo, New York, and Pittsburgh and Allentown, Pennsylvania. While many Lebanese and Syrian immigrants found employment in the steel mills of Alabama and Pennsylvania since the early 1900s, Yemeni workers, who immigrated in more recent years, are still found in large numbers at Bethlehem Steel in Buffalo, New York.

In 1951, at the age of 21, Hussein Muflahi left his home in Yemen for England. After working in England for two years, he came to Detroit, Michigan on September 14, 1953 with only a hundred dollars. After two months of working at the Ford Motor Company, he was laid off. He moved to California to work as a farm laborer in Sacramento. In 1955, he moved to Lackawanna, New York to work in the Bethlehem Steel Company. He worked there until his retirement in 1983. He lives in Buffalo with his wife, Saleha Saleh Obad, who is also from Yemen. They have ten children, 26 grandchildren, and one great grandchild. Mr. Muflahi became a U.S. citizen in 1970 and his wife was granted citizenship in 1972.

Richard Caleal (at front, left) at Studebaker, circa 1943

Richard Caleal, automotive design

Born in 1912 in Lansing, Michigan to Lebanese immigrant parents, Richard Caleal began drawing automobiles at the age of seven. Self-taught and passionate about design, he worked at Hudson, REO, Cadillac, and Packard before going to Studebaker to become a member of the famed Raymond Loewy Design Team.

In 1946, he began working as a freelance designer for George Walker, who had been awarded the contract by Henry Ford II for the design of the 1949 Ford.

Working on his kitchen table in his small bungalow in Mishawaka, Indiana, Richard designed the prototype quarter-scale model that was personally selected by Henry Ford II to become the 1949 Ford and went into production virtually unchanged.

Referred to as "The Car that Saved an Empire," the 1949 Ford helped save Ford Motor Company from financial trouble by generating an astounding $177 million profit that year. Moreover, his hyper-smooth, slab-sided design set the trend for the future of automobile styling.

Throughout the years, others tried to claim credit for Richard's revolutionary design, but in December of 2003, he was officially recognized by Ford Motor Company as the designer of the 1949 Ford.

Mahrajan

Celebrating Our Culture

Mahrajan (plural Mahrajanat) is a community festival involving music, dance, and food. Mahrajanat are held to preserve Arab culture and pass it on to younger generations. They were particularly popular among Arab American communities from the 1930s through 1960s. Beginning as small church picnics, the Mahrajanat soon grew to large outdoor events, which lasted for several days and were attended by thousands of people from all across the United States. Apart from being a space for public performances in the afternoons and evenings, they were also social events where Arab Americans got together to eat, play music, dance, make friends, and to introduce young adults to each other. The growing financial burden for the organizers led to the disappearance of these Mahrajanat in the 1970s.

Speakers at a Trenton, New Jersey Mahrajan, circa 1940

Salloum Mokarzel throwing a baseball, circa 1935

122

Resurrecting the Mahrajan

As the Mahrajanat were disappearing, Arab Americans found new ways to socialize in large gatherings. Among the most popular were the annual conventions of political, social, and professional organizations. These conventions bring together thousands of Arab Americans from around the country. The largest convention is for the Ramallah Federation, which attracts about four thousand people annually, all of whom trace their roots to the town of Ramallah in Palestine. In Michigan, hundreds of Arab American organizations hold annual banquets; the largest of which is the ACCESS dinner, which annually hosts 2,500 people.

The Mahrajan that was popular between the 1930s and 1960s is witnessing a revival in many cities. Local Arab American musicians and singers, along with singers from the Arab world, perform to large audiences. Most of these festivals are held over two to three days.

At the Arab International Festival in Dearborn, 2000

The Arab Folk Dance Group from Dearborn's Iris Becker School performs at the Arab International Festival 1996

Music and Musicians

Arab Music from Atlantic Avenue

Rashid Music Sales has been supplying Arabic music in North America for over seventy years. Established in Detroit by Albert Rashid in 1934, the company grew from its humble beginnings as a distributor of film music by Egyptian singer Mohammed Abdel Wahab to the largest supplier of Arabic music in North America. In 1947, Albert moved from Detroit to New York, where he opened his first store on Atlantic Avenue and expanded into Arabic publications, books, and periodicals. His sons, Stanley and Raymond, have carried on with the business, which has become a landmark known by musicians and artists. It attracts thousands of enthusiasts from around the world every year.

"The view I hold is that hip-hop is a mode of expression for voices that are often ignored or silenced.... I seek to represent Arab views that get little currency in the mainstream press." — Iron Sheik

Zade Dirani

Zade is a Jordanian composer and pianist known for compositions that blend Eastern Arabic scales with Western contemporary influences. He was appointed by the government of Jordan as one of the six achievers leading the country into its new era. In 2003, Zade's self-titled album stayed on the Billboard New Age charts for 13 weeks, peaking at No. 7. In the wake of September 11, 2001, Zade toured America, playing in people's living rooms, churches, temples, schools, and hospitals in a grassroots effort to create better understanding of his culture in the West. He established the Zade Dirani Foundation, aimed at helping young underprivileged musicians across the globe by offering them tangible career opportunities.

Iron Sheik

Iron Sheik is an Arab American hip-hop artist of Palestinian decent. He released his first album, "Camel Clutch 2003" in March of that year. The album features songs about politics, growing up Arab American, and bonds with other ethnic groups. Iron Sheik is just part of a growing Arab American hip-hop movement that seeks increased involvement with American politics and the arts.

Waleed Howrani

Born in New York in 1948, Waleed Howrani grew up in Beirut where he began his piano studies. At thirteen, he came to the attention of the composer Aram Khachaturian who was responsible for his scholarships to study in Moscow. Awarded the Certificate of Honor at the Tchaikovsky International Piano Competition at the age of eighteen and the Laureate in the Queen Elizabeth of Belgium Competition two years later, Waleed became a well-established concert pianist and composer.

Michele Shaheen

Jazz vocalist Michele Shaheen is renowned for her velvet-smooth vocals. Her extensive repertoire includes Cole Porter, Gershwin, and Duke Ellington. At the age of twenty, she began her professional singing career in St. Louis, Missouri and has performed with jazz greats such as guitarist Herb Ellis, trumpeter Nat Adderly, and trumpeter/vocalist Clark Terry. She won numerous awards and sang the national anthem for ABC's Monday Night Football.

Dick Dale

Known as the "King of the Surf Guitar," Dick Dale, from Lebanon, was a pioneer in the surf music of the 1950s and 60s. His style has influenced many other guitar players. His music enjoyed a great revival in the 90s with its appearances in films such as *Pulp Fiction*, *Space Jams*, and in numerous commercials.

Shakira

Shakira is the winner of the Grammy for Best Latin Pop Album and the winner of three Latin Grammy Awards. In 1999, she was named Latin Female Artists of the Year. A resident of Miami, Florida, Shakira Mebarak, is of Columbian and Lebanese descent and is influenced by music from both cultures. She gained her international fame after her 2001 hit "Whenever, Wherever."

Growing Reeds in His Backyard

Nadim Dlaikan is a Lebanese American musician and one of the leading nay players in the United States. He is recognized by his peers for the significant contributions he has made to the artistic life of the Arab American community in Michigan. He received the Michigan Heritage Award in 1994 and the prestigious Kennedy Center's National Heritage Fellowship in 2002.

Nadim developed his great fondness for the nay from his uncle, learning to play on a flute he stole from his brother. When his family took his nay away from him, his response was to learn to make his own flutes using locally available reeds.

He first performed in his home village and later in Beirut. Eventually moving to Cairo, he connected with several international folk troupes. After touring with Samira Tawfik, a famous Egyptian singer, Nadim came to the United States, finally settling in Dearborn. In 1992, he founded the Dearborn Traditional Arabic Ensemble, which includes some of the top musicians available in the area. The group conserves the traditional musical genres found in Arabic music and shares the music with diverse audiences around the world. Nadim is also committed to teaching and preserving the music of the nay. He continues to make his own instruments by growing reeds in his backyard and drying them to create a variety of Arab flutes.

Arab Americans in the Military

Arab Americans have been serving in the U.S. military since the Revolutionary War, and they fought during the American Civil War in both the Confederate Army and the Union Army.

During World War I, Arab American community leaders urged young Arab American men to join the U.S. armed forces in order to help their new country. According to military records, at least 13,965, or about seven percent, of the Syrian community served in the army.

Subsequent wars and military operations in which Arab Americans served include: World War II; Korea; Vietnam; the U.S. Multinational Force [USMNF] in Beirut, Lebanon and Kosovo. They also served in the 1991 Iraq Gulf War, U.S. war in Afghanistan after 9/11/2001; and the 2002 Iraq war.

Currently, there are thousands of Arab Americans serving in the U.S. Armed Forces. These men and women are willing to sacrifice their lives for the protection and defense of the United States of America, its constitution, freedoms, and citizens. Arab Americans are found in every rank and division of the military. The Association of Patriotic Arab Americans in Military (APAAM) serves to connect Arab Americans serving in the military with each other.

Maintaining Morale: "The Journal"

The Knights of St. George published its first issue of "The Journal" in May 1944 for the purpose of communicating with Syrian and Lebanese men who were serving in World War II. This effort was made possible by the generous support and encouragement of Arab American Mr. J. K. Samara.

The journal provided servicemen stationed throughout the world the opportunity to learn the whereabouts of friends and brothers. In many instances reunions were thus possible. Communication and reuniting were the source of inestimable joy and increase in morale to the men and to the readers who shared their experiences through the "Letters to the Editor."

HEADQUARTERS 1ST BN-331ST ENGINEERS

Group X, APO 462
Minneapolis, Minn
April 24, 1943.

Mrs. Sarah Said
1696 Salian St
Dearborne, Mich.

Dear Madam:

I am enclosing a letter of Commendation received from General H. L. George of the United States Army, which was addressed to your son Allie Said.

This letter was received since your son has been missing and as it is a letter of worthy praise coming from a high ranking United States Officer, I am happy to enclose it for your keeping.

Very truly yours,

Felix A. Davis
FELIX A DAVIS
1st Lt-CE

ARMY AIR FORCES
HEADQUARTERS, AIR TRANSPORT COMMAND
WASHINGTON

SUBJECT: Letter of Commendation.   February 4, 1943.

TO: 1st Sergeant Ali Said
           (THROUGH: Commanding Officer, Alaskan Wing)

1. Details of the rescue of Lt. Joseph P. Donahue have recently been brought to my attention. In this connection, I wish to take this opportunity to commend you for your efforts and the part you played in rescuing Lt. Donahue.

2. Your heroic hike over the trails for some twelve hours under most trying sub-zero temperatures unquestionably helped to save the life of one of our ferry pilots.

3. This command takes due cognizance of the role that you have played and commends you for your action.

H. L. George
H. L. GEORGE
Major General, U. S. A.
Commanding.

In Loving Memory of

First Sergeant
ALLIE JOSEPH SAID

For country and his flag he fought
 Upon the battlefield,
With proven courage he strode on
 Nor would he ever yield
Until the great Commander called
 The brave one to come home
For a promotion to the skies
 From which he shall not roam;
So now he sleeps beneath his flag
 But we will shed no tear
For from his courage we shall learn
 To have no thought of fear.

Notable Service

Navy Lieutenant Alfred Naifeh was promoted to Lieutenant in 1942. That year, while he was serving on the USS Meredith in the Solomon Islands, the ship was struck by the Japanese in an air raid. He worked for two days and nights to locate his wounded shipmates and get them aboard life rafts. On the third day, he died of exhaustion. He was posthumously awarded the Navy and Marine Corps Medal and the Purple Heart for his heroism. In 1944, one of the U.S. Navy ships, the destroyer USS Naifeh, was named in his honor.

Colonel James Jabara, America's first Jet Ace, is best known for his outstanding record of enemy takedowns during the Korean Conflict.

Born in Oklahoma, Jabara's career reflected the dedicated work ethic and patriotism typical of first-generation Arab Americans. A devoted serviceman, he flew over 100 combat missions during World War II. An airport in Wichita, Kansas is named after him.

Brigadier General William Jabour is Vice Commander, Aeronautical Systems Center, Air Force Materiel Command, at Wright-Patterson Air Force Base, Ohio. He entered the military service in 1973 and later worked as an experimental test pilot for various aircrafts. His major awards and decorations include a Legion of Merit, a Defense Meritorious Service Medal, and a Meritorious Service Medal with Three Oak Leaf Clusters, an Air Force Commendation Medal, and an Air Force Achievement Medal with Oak Leaf Cluster. In 2000, he was made director of the F-22 System Program Office (SPO) at Air Force Materiel Command's Aeronautical Systems Center (ASC) at Wright-Patterson AFB, Ohio.

General George Joulwan held the highest military position in NATO, the Supreme Allied Commander, in Europe (SACEUR). Under this title, he oversaw NATO's military operations in Bosnia. President Bill Clinton said of Joulwan, "His efforts have built a foundation for a Europe that is safe, secure, and democratic well into the 21st century."

Major General L. Massad
Nicknamed "Iron Mike" for his athletic abilities during his years at the University of Oklahoma. Massad was not only an accomplished football player, but also a World War II veteran. He retired from the U.S. Army as a Major General in 1968. His honors include the Distinguished Service Medal, a Silver Star, Legion of Merit, a Bronze Star with Oak Leaf Cluster, Purple Heart, Silver Arrow Head, and the Presidential Unit Citation. He also served as Deputy Assistant Secretary of Defense under President Lyndon Johnson.

Lieutenant Colonel Ahmed M. Ragheb
Command pilot and member of a three-man crew that set the world record for flying between Tokyo and Los Angles in eight hours and twenty-seven minutes, Ragheb served for 29 years in the U.S. Air Forces. An Egyptian who came to the United States at age 15, Lt. Colonel Ragheb served in Desert Storm and later held diplomatic assignments in Saudi Arabia, Egypt, Yemen, and Sudan.

Arab American Journalism

In 1892, Najeeb Arbeely, a founding father of Arab American journalism, published the first Arabic newspaper in the United States, *Kawkab Amirka* (*Star of America*). The newspaper, written in both Arabic and English, reported stories from the Arab American community in New York as well as news from the Arab world. In 1894, Na'uum Mokarzel began *Al-Asr* (*Contemporary Times* or *The Midday*) newspaper. Four years later, he began another newspaper, *Al-Hoda* (*The Guidance*) with his brother, Salloum. Many local newspapers followed and by 1907, twenty-one Arabic newspapers had been established in various cities. By 1930, their number had grown to fifty.

Early Arabic newspapers allowed Arab American communities to stay connected to the Arab world and helped early immigrants adjust to their new life in the United States. However, the growth of newspapers in the Arabic language slowed down after World War I as new laws restricted the entry of immigrants, and only a few Arab Americans born in the United States could read Arabic. In the 1920s, Arab Americans began to publish newspapers in English only, such as *The Syrian World*, but continued to report on issues important to the Arab American community. Today, hundreds of Arab American newspapers are published. Most are bilingual and address local issues, as well as provide a perspective different from that of American newspapers on international events.

Afifa Karem

Afifa Karem was the first well-known Arab American female journalist. Born in Lebanon, she immigrated to the United States in 1897 with her husband at the age of fourteen. Four years later, she began writing articles for Arabic newspapers and journals such as *Al-Hoda* and *The Syrian Woman*. Much of her writing argued for the rights of Arab and American women. She was also the publisher and editor of the magazine *The New World*, a ladies monthly Arabic magazine.

Al-Hoda

Naoum and Salloum Mokarzel, the founders of *Al-Hoda* newspaper, and their successors, Mary Mokarzel and Fares Stephen, made *Al-Hoda (The Guidance)* one of the most important Arabic newspapers published in the United States. In February of 1898, *Al-Hoda* became a weekly publication out of Philadelphia until 1903, when the Mokarzel brothers moved to New York and published *Al-Hoda* as a daily paper. Covering news from the Arab world and the United States, *Al-Hoda* provided a forum for the discussion of social, cultural, and political issues.

Anthony Shadid

The grandson of Lebanese immigrants, Anthony Shadid received the 2004 Pulitzer Prize for International Reporting. The Prize was awarded to him for his coverage of the Iraq war and his outstanding ability to capture the stories of ordinary Iraqis. Shadid is currently the *Washington Post* correspondent for Islamic affairs in the Arab world. During a previous assignment at the *Boston Globe*, Shadid was shot and seriously wounded while covering the Palestinian-Israeli conflict.

In *Al Jadid: A Review & Record of Arab Culture and Arts*, a quarterly magazine published in Los Angeles, editor and founder Elie Chalala keeps his readers abreast of current aesthetic trends among Arab and Arab American writers and artists. Published in English, the colorful magazine includes reviews of books, films, and music, as well as interviews with contemporary artists and writers.

Arab American Literature and Writers: In Our Own Words

In 1923, Arab American literature became popular with the immediate success of *The Prophet* by Khalil Gibran. Along with two other Lebanese American poets, Amin Rihany and Mikhail Naimy, Gibran formed *al-Rabitah al-Qalamiyyah, (The Pen League)*. Writing in both Arabic and English, these authors were dedicated to regenerating the Arabic language and freeing literature from the constraints of tradition through modern poetry.

Today, Arab American literature includes memoirs, essays, poetry, short stories, and novels. Writers such as Edward Said, Fawaz Turki, and Leila Ahmed have shared their life stories of coming to America. Khalid Mattawa and Naomi Shihab Nye continue the tradition of Arab American poetry as a vibrant form of expression. Editors Marilyn Booth and Salyma Khadra Jayyusi have made contemporary Arabic fiction accessible through their English translations.

Influenced by *A Thousand and One Nights* and American writers such as William Faulkner, contemporary Arab American novelists bring together the richness of both American and Arab cultures. Female novelists Kathryn K. Abdul-Baki, Diane Abu-Jaber, and Laila Hallaby depict their characters traveling between the Arab world and America as their novels explore the problems and hopes faced by Arab Americans. Through the efforts of these writers and many more, Arab American literature has claimed its place in the canon of modern American literature.

Stereotypes

The stereotypes used in depicting Arab Americans are rooted in what scholar Edward Said called Orientalism, the process by which the West portrays Eastern culture as morally inferior. In the eighteenth and nineteenth centuries, European Orientalist artists and writers presented the Arab world as heathen and savage, casting the region as exotic and ill-reputed while neglecting to recognize the region's contributions to human civilization.

Throughout the twentieth century, American stereotypes of the Arab world and Arab Americans moved from elite realms of art and literature into popular culture. Negative images of Arabs have been sustained through songs, television programs, film, consumer products, comic strips, and national news media. These portrayals have become ingrained into the public consciousness, resulting in real and lasting consequences.

Media analyst Jack Shaheen reviewed over one thousand movies spanning the beginning of film until the present. Of all the films, fifty portrayed Arabs evenhandedly, and only twelve contained positive Arab depictions. Hollywood and the media have repeatedly reinforced, recreated, and perpetuated images of barbarians, villains, seducers, sheiks, belly dancers, and terrorists.

The harmful influences of stereotypes depend not only on the repetition of negative imagery, but also the omission of positive imagery. What is absent are the important images of Arab Americans who made lasting contributions to society as local business owners, family members, teachers, classmates, artists, engineers, and neighbors.

This room includes two large walls that stand on either side of a video projection. The walls show historical and more recent stereotypical depictions, while the video presents a series of street interviews. On the opposite side of the room images of the real, everyday people whom negative images aim to degrade are portrayed, along with a collage of illustrations showing Arabs and Arab Americans contemplating their self-image as they actively take charge of establishing a positive, self-determined identity in an intensity of activity and creativity.

Created by OTHER: Arab artists collective.

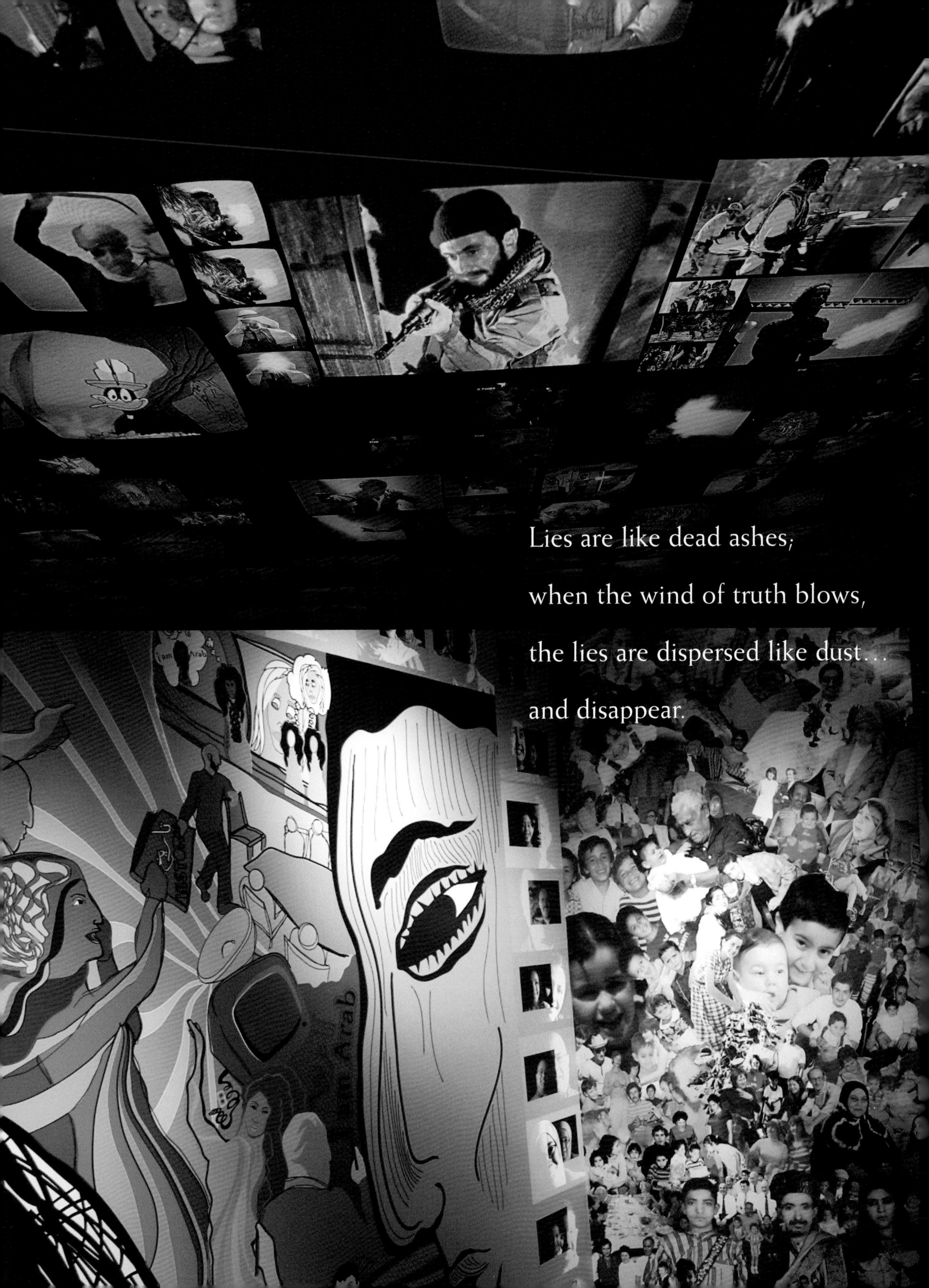

Lies are like dead ashes;

when the wind of truth blows,

the lies are dispersed like dust…

and disappear.

Becoming American

The United States is one of the most diverse nations in the world. Except for the Native Americans, every American can trace his or her background to some other place. While Europeans were the first to settle in North America, other groups followed. Over the years, the United States government created various regulations and immigration laws in order to control who can visit, work, or study in the United States or become a U.S. citizen.

Pledging allegiance to the American Flag after becoming citizens on November 26, 2004

U.S. Citizenship

U.S. citizenship is granted to individuals either by right of birth or through naturalization. Citizenship is automatically granted to those born in the United States or to children of U.S. citizens, even if they are born outside the country. Naturalization is the process of granting citizenship to foreigners born outside the United States.

General requirements for naturalization:

1. Demonstrable period of continuous residence and physical presence in the United States after having been admitted as a permanent resident
2. The ability to read, write, and speak English
3. A knowledge and understanding of U.S. history and government
4. Good moral character
5. An attachment to the principles of the U.S. Constitution
6. A favorable disposition toward the United States

Green Card

A Green Card entitles its holder to live, work, and study permanently in the United States, as well as enter and leave the country freely. Green Card holders have access to health care, education, social security benefits, and are subject to federal and state taxes. Although a Green Card does not necessarily guarantee U.S. citizenship, it is a prerequisite to naturalization.

Those who want to immigrate to the United States must have their sponsoring relatives or employers submit an application on their behalf to Citizenship and Immigration Services (formerly the Immigration and Naturalization Service). Upon approval, their application is transferred to the State Department for review and visa issuance at their local American Embassy or Consulate abroad. The State Department grants immigrant visas on the basis of specific quotas allocated to each country, giving priority to special skills, family unification, or investments. Under specific circumstances some individuals are granted asylum and refugee visas, or given temporary protection status. Immigrant visas for certain immediate relatives of petitioning U.S. citizens, however, are unlimited. Additionally, an annual Green Card lottery provides 55,000 randomly selected foreign citizens immigrant visas.

Nonimmigrant Visa

A nonimmigrant visa allows a foreign citizen to temporarily visit or work in the United States. There are a variety of nonimmigrant visa categories (more than forty), differing in privileges offered and duration of stay. They include tourist, work, and medical visas.

"I felt like a citizen for 82 years"

After living in the United States for 82 years, **Mary Korkmas** finally took the Oath of Allegiance to become an American citizen on June 25th, 1986. She had arrived at Ellis Island from Greater Syria with her mother in 1904, when she was just three years old. Unfortunately, the 1916 fire at Ellis Island destroyed her entry papers, along with countless others. However, it was not until 1950 that she realized that she was not a citizen! After three failed attempts to gain her citizenship, she turned her attention towards raising her family in Texas. In 1984, she met her friend, Gayla Lawson, who helped her with the citizenship process. Mary said that although she only officially became a U.S. citizen at the age of 85, she felt like a citizen for 82 years.

Chapter Three
Making An Impact

Over the past century, Arab American contributions have enriched the political, economic, and cultural life in the United States. Arab Americans have risen to prominence in every profession.

Community

They are inventors and innovators; they are doctors and engineers; they are entrepreneurs, scientists, politicians, activists, and entertainers. They are immigrants, children, and grandchildren of immigrants, whose hard work, determination, creativity, and commitment made it possible for them to succeed in their professions. Their achievements are as multifaceted as the communities from which they have emerged.

The list of Arab American individuals and organizations that have positively impacted our lives is long and distinguished. And for every individual who has become a leader in his or her field, there are thousands of others whose unacknowledged contributions continue to enrich the lives of all Americans.

Sting and Her Majesty Queen Noor at the 2001 Khalil Gibran Spirit Award

ACCESS Executive Director Ismael Ahmed discusses welfare reform and immigration matters with President William J. Clinton in 1995.

Arab Community Center for Economic and Social Service (ACCESS)

ACCESS is a nonprofit organization committed to the development of the Arab American community in all aspects of its life. Since 1971, the organization has grown from a humble storefront office run by a small group of volunteers to an agency with seventy different programs and an annual budget of over $12 million by 2005. In 1992, President George H. W. Bush designated ACCESS to receive a "Points of Light" Award as an exemplary nonprofit organization. In 1995, the United Way of Southeastern Michigan named ACCESS's Executive Director Ismael Ahmed the "Director of the Year" and in 2000, the organization won the *Crain's Detroit Business* annual competition for the "Best Managed Non-Profit."

While ACCESS is the first and oldest of the Arab American human service institutions, there are many Arab American groups across the country doing similar work, including: Arab American & Chaldean Council in Detroit, American Arab Heritage Council in Flint, Arab Cultural Center in San Francisco, Arab American Action Network in Chicago, Arab American Community Center in Orlando, Arab American Community Center for Economic and Social Services in Cleveland, Arab American Cultural and Community Center in Houston, Arab American Family Support Center in Brooklyn, ACCESS California Services in Anaheim, Arab American Community Development Corporation in Philadelphia, Arab American Association of New York, and Arab American Family Services in Chicago.

American Federation of Ramallah, Palestine, known as the Ramallah Federation

Did you know that there are more people from Ramallah, Palestine in the United States than in Ramallah itself? The Ramallah Federation, which was founded in 1959, has its headquarters in Detroit, Michigan and has chapters in various cities throughout the United States.

The goal of the federation is "the unity of the Ramallah family," which builds on the tradition of extended family and strong ties within one's village. It seeks to perpetuate and strengthen those ties for individuals from Ramallah living in the United States. The federation holds annual conventions that are attended by four thousand to five thousand participants.

Members of the Ramallah Federation attending the first hafleh at the organization's first convention in Detroit, Michigan. 1959.

Palestine Aid Society of America (PAS)

The Palestinian struggle and aspiration for national independence has been an issue of concern to most Arab Americans and has motivated the political and cultural organization of many of them in the United States. In 1978, the Palestine Aid Society of America was established to provide material and political support for the Palestinian people in the occupied territories and Lebanon. Through its chapters in various U.S. cities, the organization held a variety of cultural and educational activities that help the general public develop a more comprehensive understanding of the Palestinian struggle to end the occupation and build an independent state.

During the 1970s and 1980s, many other Palestinian American organizations emerged to support the same cause, such the United Holy Land Fund, Roots, and Palestine Solidarity Committee.

The Federation of Islamic Associations in the United States and Canada

While in the Army during World War II, Abdallah Igram recognized the extent to which Islam was misinterpreted among his fellow servicemen. Many Arab American Muslims shared his view and wanted Americans at large to better understand and respect their religion. As a result, Igram and other Arab American Muslims came together to create an organization that would achieve equal recognition for American Muslims.

In 1952, the Federation of Islamic Association in the United States and Canada was founded in Cedar Rapids, Iowa. The federation held annual conventions and gave special attention to the spirit, ethics, and culture of Islam for Muslims and their children.

From the Newsweek article "Mr. Muslim in America"

On a Federation of Islamic Associations in the United States visit to Egypt with then president Gamal Abdel Nasser

Arab American Institute (AAI)

Founded in 1985 by James J. Zogby and George R. Salem, the Arab American Institute (AAI) is a non-profit organization committed to the civic and political empowerment of Americans of Arab descent. The AAI provides leadership training and strategies in electoral politics and policy issues. In addition to registering and organizing Arab American voters, the institute serves as a clearinghouse for community participation in national, state, and local politics. The AAI is affiliated with the AAI Foundation, which supports information and education programs on the role and contributions of Arab Americans, and the Arab American Leadership Council (ALC), a national network of Arab Americans serving in elected or appointed office. Through these affiliations, AAI has become a resource for research on the Arab American constituency and community concerns.

At the Texas State Republican Convention

Arab American
Republicans
for
Victory in '92

American-Arab Anti-Discrimination Committee (ADC)

Frustrated by the stereotyping and discrimination experienced by Arab Americans, Senator James Abourezk established the ADC in 1980. With chapters nationwide, it is the largest Arab American civil rights organization in the United States.

The ADC defends Arab Americans who are victims of discrimination and challenges the media and other institutions that provide misinformation about their culture. Since its establishment, the committee has defended thousands of Arab Americans who have been discriminated against because of their religion or national origin. The committee's work has increased dramatically since September 11, 2001.

Syrian Ladies Aid Society of New York

Few things could be more frightening than arriving at a new country where the resources are limited, the contacts are few, and the surrounding voices are difficult to understand. For these reasons and in an effort to provide financial, medical, and support services to young Syrian girls and women arriving at the Port of New York, twelve young women of Syrian descent joined together in a voluntary association, the Syrian Ladies Aid Society of New York, in 1907.

According to their constitution and bylaws, early members paid $10 annually in dues. Although this amount was humble, the organization succeeded in giving more than that to the needy, aged, infirm, and young. The organization grew to donate thousands of dollars to individuals and various organizations in New York City and the nation. After ninety-three years of service, the organization dissolved in the year 2000.

Syrian Ladies Aid Society dinner, held at Prospect Hall on March 15, 1912

SYRIAN LADIES AID SOCIETY.
PROSPECT·HALL
MAR. 15.1912

Community Initiative: The Building of the Kahlil

Recognizing that Gibran's strong belief in the reconciliation of sectarian strife in Lebanon could be a strong symbol for peace, Sheryl Fiegel and Khalil Haddad explored the idea of creating a sculpture of Kahlil Gibran in Washington, D.C. as a tribute to Arab Americans. Their vision of creating a memorial garden with a Gibran statue was a major undertaking that required an act of the U.S. Congress. Only one in two hundred proposals such as this ever make it through the legislative process. Joint resolutions introduced into the Senate by Sen. George Mitchell and into the House by Congressman Abraham Kazen received substantial bipartisan support from fifty members of Congress and twenty-five senators. In 1983, on the 100th anniversary of Kahlil Gibran's birthday, the Kahlil Gibran Centennial Foundation was incorporated, chaired by former President Jimmy Carter.

On October 19, 1984, President Ronald Reagan signed the bill. A site on Massachusetts Avenue near the home of the Vice President of the United States was chosen from among thirteen possible locations.

Beginning in the late 1980s, William J. Baroody Jr. became Chairman of the Memorial, which raised the necessary funding that brought the project to fruition. Under the leadership of Mr. Baroody and the Foundation board, a small staff, many hard-working volunteers and generous donors, a memorial garden, featuring a sculptural component designed by Washington-based sculptor Gordon Kray, was dedicated during Memorial Day weekend, 1991 by President George H. W. Bush.

"Hundreds of years later, when the people of the city arose from the slumber of ignorance and saw the dawn of knowledge, they erected a monument in the most beautiful garden of the city and celebrated a feast every year in honor of that poet, whose writings had freed them. Oh how cruel is man's ignorance." —From Gibran's *The Poet's Death Is His Life*

Arab Chamber of Commerce

The American Arab Chamber of Commerce, founded in 1992 in Detroit, Michigan, was a driving force for the development of Arab chambers in many cities across the United States. Established to better serve the Arab American business communities, these chambers promote, assist, and strengthen member businesses in the domestic and international arenas. The chambers provide business referrals, member promotion, networking events, information exchange through their publications, and serve as the voice of their members with lawmakers and governmental agencies.

In order to access the lucrative Arab American markets, a growing number of businesses are joining these chambers, since membership allows businesses to expand their market base. From the mom-and-pop stores to large international corporations, chamber members receive many benefits designed to improve business operations and boost profits.

Founding Chairman Ned Fawaz, Chairman Ahmed Chebbani, Board Member Jessica Pelegrno, 2002 National Business Man of the Year, Wedge Group Chairman Nijad Fares Fares, and Chamber Executive Director Nasser Beydoun at the 10th Annual Chamber of Commerce Banquet

American Task Force for Lebanon

The American Task Force of Lebanon (ATFL), a nonprofit, nonpartisan organization located in Washington, D.C., was founded as part of the National Association of Arab Americans in 1987 during a time of great crisis in Lebanon. As many Arab Americans are of Lebanese ancestry, it was hoped that the resources of prominent Lebanese Americans could be marshaled to assist, direct, and persuade the various United States government entities to provide much-needed assistance to Lebanon. The goal of the ATFL has evolved into strengthening United States-Lebanon relations on a number of different tracks.

The leadership of the ATFL has included: Mr. Peter J. Tanous, The Hon. Thomas A. Nassif, Nijad I. Fares, The Hon. Darrell Issa, The Hon. Edward M. Gabriel, Mr. Richard A. Abdoo, Dr. Joseph Jacob, Ms. Tanya Rahall, and Dr. George T. Cody.

The Honorable Thomas A. Nassif, ATFL Chairman

Did You Know? This Arab American is the founder and president of Alamo Flag Company, which is the largest flag retailer in the United States. He has donated part of Alamo's earnings to families of the victims of the September 11, 2001 attacks and is designing and manufacturing a flag with images of the World Trade Center and Pentagon *(answer on following page)*

Making an Impact: Activism

Candace Lightner gives Ronald Reagan a MADD pin

Addes being carried by supporters

Candace Lightner

Founder of Mothers Against Drunk Driving (MADD), Candace Lightner served as Chief Executive Officer, President, and Chairperson of the Board for five and a half years. In less than three years, she expanded MADD into an international corporation with approximately four hundred chapters worldwide and an annual budget of over $12 million. Recognizing her years of dynamic leadership, the media voted her one of the most influential American citizens of the twentieth century.

George Addes

George Addes was one of the most prominent Arab American labor activists and a leader in the formation of the United Auto Workers (UAW) during the 1930s. Under his leadership, the union grew from fewer than thirty thousand members to half a million. Born in Wisconsin, Addes was forced to leave school and support his family at age 17. Working as a wet-sander for 65 cents a day, he led a workers' organization to demand better wages and working conditions. In 1936, UAW members elected him as the first Secretary-Treasurer of the UAW-CIO, a position he held for ten consecutive terms.

Answer: Tony Ismail: entrepreneur

Steve Yokich

A community leader and trade unionist, Yokich dedicated his forty-six-year career to economic empowerment and social justice. Born in Detroit to a Lebanese mother and a Greek father, he grew up in a U.A.W. home as both his parents were active union members. Throughout his life he was a dedicated trade unionist and in 1977 became regional director of the U.A.W. In 1980, he was elected international Vice President and then President in 1995. Yokich is credited with repairing relations with General Motors Corporation after the 1998 strikes in Flint and successfully negotiating Election Day as a paid holiday for union members.

Yokich

Richard C. Shadyac

Richard C. Shadyac was an early supporter of Danny Thomas' efforts to found St. Jude Children's Research Hospital. For thirteen years he was the National Executive Director of the American Lebanese Syrian Associated Charities (ALSAC), which is the fund-raising department of St. Jude's Children's Research Hospital and is one of the nation's largest heath care charities. A dedicated social activist, Shadyac is also the cofounder of the National Association of Arab Americans and the Arab American Association. Prior to joining ALSAC, he was a trial lawyer for the Department of Justice.

Shadyac

Shadid, at left, laying the cornerstone at Community Hospital, 1929

Michael Shadid

Known as a "Doctor for the People," Dr. Michael Shadid pioneered America's first cooperative hospital, Community Hospital, in the farming community of Elk City, Oklahoma in 1929. Born in Syria, he came to the United States as a teenager and worked as a peddler selling jewelry to support his medical studies at the University of Washington in St. Louis. Today, the Great Plains Regional Medical Center continues to carry out his mission by providing patients with comprehensive, cost-effective, and high quality heath care.

Hassan

Hagopian

Jabara

Menconi

Aliya Hassan

A leading political and community activist until her death in 1990, Aliya Hassan was a guiding force in the establishment and growth of the Arab Community Service for Economic and Social Services (ACCESS). She was born in South Dakota in 1910 to two of the first Lebanese Muslims to arrive in the United States. Her activism extended beyond the Arab American community. A close friend to Malcolm X, she organized his first trip to Mecca and led a group of African American leaders on a trip to Egypt to meet with President Gamal Abdel Nasser.

Elaine Hagopian

Elaine Hagopian is one of the foremost Arab American activists and scholars in the field of Arab American studies. Professor Emeritus at Simmons College in Boston, she was a founding member of the Arab American University Graduates and the principal founder of the Trans-Arab Research Institute. A member of the advisory board of Al-Awda (The Palestine Right to Return Coalition), Hagopian organized their first major conference, "Right of Return: Palestinian Refugees and a Durable Peace," held at Boston University in 2000. Her work successfully bridges the gap between activism and scholarship.

Abdeen Jabara

A prominent civil rights attorney, Abdeen Jabara played a key role in exposing the U.S. government's Operation Boulder, a program that began in the 1960s and involved activities such as surveillance and deportation of Arabs and Arab Americans. He is a founding member of the Association of Arab American University Graduates and was President of the American-Arab Anti-Discrimination Committee from 1986 until 1990.

Evelyn Menconi

Evelyn Menconi dedicated her life to actively promoting Arab American culture through her curatorial work at the William G. Abdalah Memorial Library, established in her brother's memory, and as an educational consultant for the cable television show, *The Arabic Hour*. A life-long educator in the Boston Public School system, she received her doctorate in education at age sixty from Boston University.

Saving the South End, Dearborn, Michigan

The "South End," which developed as the center of the much wider Metro Detroit Arab American community, struggled for its existence in the decades of the 1970s and 1980s. As the first step in implementing its Master Plan of transforming the densely populated neighborhood from residential to industrial, the City of Dearborn began to demolish residential homes during the late sixties. Leaders of the community formed the Southeast Dearborn Community Council and initiated a legal action in Federal Court. Spanning over seventeen years, the *Amen et al. vs. the City of Dearborn et al.* case was filed in 1971 and resulted in an overwhelming victory for the South End in 1988. The court found the city's actions in violation of the community's civil rights and a denial of due process of law. The struggle was significant in its development of political awareness and grassroots participation among Dearborn's Arab American community. The South End neighborhood has grown and prospered since then, never losing the "sense of community" it established during the campaign to "Save the South End."

Ralph Nader

A presidential candidate in 1996, 2000, and 2004, Ralph Nader is the United States' leading consumer advocate. Born in Connecticut, he began his career as a lawyer in Hartford in 1959. He first made headlines in 1965 with his book, *Unsafe at Any Speed*, an indictment of the auto industry for producing unsafe vehicles. The book successfully led to the passage in 1966 of a series of automobile safety laws. In his career as a lawyer, author, and consumer advocate, Nader founded many organizations, including the Center for Responsive Law, the Public Interest Research Group, the Center for Auto Safety, Public Citizen Clean Water Action Project, the Disability Rights Center, the Pension Rights Center, and the Project for Corporate Responsibility.

Dr. Hala Maksoud

Dr. Hala Maksoud came to the United States in 1974 with her husband, Dr. Clovis Maksoud. She was a tireless activist for Arab Americans, one of the founders of the American-Arab Anti-Discrimination Committee and Washington's Arab Women's Council. In addition to serving as president of both organizations, she worked with the American Committee on Jerusalem, Committee for the Preservation of Palestinian Heritage, and Arab American University Graduates. She also taught at Georgetown University's Center for Contemporary Arab Studies.

Nader

Maksoud

Did You Know? Ed Masry is an attorney and environmentalist who is perhaps best known for helping a famous activist win $333 million from Pacific Gas and Electric after discovering that the utility was poisoning the community's drinking water. Their story was made into a film starring Oscar-winning actress Julia Roberts. What was the film? *(answer on following page)*

Making an Impact: Science

Najjar taking a blood sample in Dembia Plain in Ethiopia. Upon pricking her finger for vaccination, the woman covered her face impulsively.

Dr. Abdallah E. Najjar

Dr. Abdallah E. Najjar has traveled the world working with the U.S. government to eradicate malaria, including military assignments in Iran and Ethiopia. First in his class at Universal College of Aley in Lebanon, he immigrated to the United States and served in the Third Army Division, Special Troops medical battalion during World War II. After a long career in international service, he worked as chief of Atlanta's Communicable Disease Center International Affairs office. A lifelong proponent of the global eradication of disease, Dr. Najjar once said, "Only by direct involvement can we measure up to our responsibilities. Disease knows no boundaries and the world is getting smaller."

Dr. Ahmed H. Zewail

The recipient of numerous awards for his scientific achievements, Dr. Ahmed Zewail received the Nobel Prize in Chemistry in 1999 for his work as the pioneer of femtochemistry, the study of chemical reactions across femtoseconds. The California Institute of Technology professor was born in Egypt, where postage stamps were issued to honor his contributions to science and humanity. He received his first degree from the University of Alexandria before moving from Egypt to the United States to complete his Ph.D. at the University of Pennsylvania.

Christa McAuliffe

On January 28, 1986, Christa McAuliffe embarked on what she called "the ultimate field trip." The Concord High School Social Studies teacher had been chosen from a pool of 11,500 applicants to become the first civilian in space. Tragically, her life ended when the Challenger Space Shuttle exploded shortly after takeoff. In 1990, the Christa McAuliffe Planetarium opened in Concord, New Hampshire to fulfill her motto: "I touch the future, I teach."

Zewail

McAuliffe

NASA

CHRISTA

Answer: *Erin Brockovich*

Doumani

Dr. George Doumani

A veteran of five scientific expeditions to Antarctica, Dr. George Doumani is the only Arab American, to date, to have explored the continent's interior. His research as a geologist helped prove the theory of continental drift. In his honor, there are two geographical features in Antarctica named after him by the National Board of Geographic Names: Mount Doumani and Doumani Peak.

Dr. Omar Alfi

Dr. Omar Alfi is a leader in the field of genetics. In the early 1970s, he identified a rare chromosome anomaly now known as the Alfi Syndrome, which causes mental and physical developmental delays. In 1981, he established the first private, full-service cytogenetics laboratory in Pasadena, California. One of the largest independent genetics laboratories, Alfigen Inc. provides the highest quality services to the medical community. An avid philanthropist, Dr. Alfi established the Aldeen Foundation, a nonprofit organization that sponsors teacher conferences, provides scholarships, develops curriculums in Arabic, and supports the Arabic language book collection in the four Aldeen libraries. He and his wife also endowed the Omar and Azmeralda Alfi Distinguished Fellowship in Islamic Law at the University of California, Los Angeles.

Alfi

Dr. Elias Zerhouni

In 2002, Dr. Elias Zerhouni was named director of the National Institutes of Health. Born in Nedroma, Algeria, he spoke very little English when he arrived in the United States at age twenty-four in 1975, yet he went on to successfully complete his residency in diagnostic radiology at Johns Hopkins University. He is a member of the National Academy of Sciences' Institute of Medicine and serves on the National Cancer Institute's Board of Scientific Advisors. In 1988, he was a consultant to the World Health Organization, and in 1985, he acted as consultant to the White House under President Ronald Reagan.

Hand-stitched Lebanese Flag Circa 1958. Made by Dr. Doumani and flown from his Sno-Cat while traversing the Antarctic continent. He sought to acquire a Lebanese flag before leaving on his exposition, but departed before it arrived. Determined, he made this one using his pillow case and two pieces of red cloth that were used as trail markers. He enlarged the cedar tree from a postage stamp, drafted it in the center of the flag, and painted it with green India ink.

Zerhouni

Elachi

El Baz

Massab

Dr. Charles Elachi

Dr. Charles Elachi is best known for helping to develop a series of imaging radar systems for space shuttles that allow scientists to see through the clouds that blanket the Earth. Born in 1947 in Lebanon, the Caltech professor was named director of the Jet Propulsion Laboratory in 2001. He has served as principle investigator for numerous NASA flight projects, research, and development studies. In 1989, Asteroid 1982 SU was renamed 4116 Elachi in recognition of his contributions to planetary exploration.

Hassan Al-Sabbah

Inventor Hassan Al-Sabbah came to the United States in 1921 from Nabatieh, Lebanon and earned a Master's degree in Engineering Sciences from the University of Illinois. In 1923, General Electric hired him to work in its Engineering Laboratory under a contract that awarded him a dollar for each of his patents. Between 1927 and 1935, he invented fifty-two different applications for his patents at GE.

Dr. Farouk El Baz

When the astronauts of Apollo 15 circled the moon for the first time, they felt they were in familiar territory, thanks to the training of Dr. Farouk El Baz, who from 1968 to 1972 helped plan the Apollo moon landings and pioneered the use of space photography to study Earth. His research is also used to understand arid terrain and locate groundwater resources. Since 1986, the Egyptian-born scientist has worked as the director of the Center for Remote Sensing at Boston University.

Dr. John Massab

Dr. John Massab is the inventor of FluMist, a revolutionary nasal spray flu vaccine that is distributed worldwide. Professor Emeritus of Epidemiology at the University of Michigan's School of Public Health, Dr. Massab dedicated forty years to research in public health before FluMist received FDA approval in July 2003.

Dr. George Hatem

One of the most famous foreign doctors in China, Dr. Hatem earned the distinction for his work in helping the Chinese stamp out venereal disease. The son of Lebanese immigrants, he was born in Buffalo, New York and obtained a medical degree at the University of Geneva in Switzerland. In 1933, he moved to China, where he lived out the rest of his life and was the first non-Chinese to gain citizenship in the People's Republic of China.

Dr. Rashid Bashshur

Dr. Rashid Bashshur, a professor at the University of Michigan's School of Public Health, is a pioneer and leading international expert in the field of telemedicine, which has been defined as the "use of telecommunications to provide medical information and services." This technology is broadly defined as anything from a telephone exchange between two medical practitioners, to using satellite technology and videoconferencing equipment for medical consultation between doctors in two different continents. Telemedicine is now practiced in all U.S. states and most countries around the globe.

Community Initiative:
Founding of St. Jude Children's Research Hospital

The inspiration for St. Jude Children's Research Hospital came from the patron saint of hopeless causes, whom Danny Thomas asked for help while struggling to launch his career in entertainment. Funding for the hospital's annual operations comes from the American Lebanese Syrian Associated Charities (ALSAC). After raising the money to build the hospital, Thomas turned to fellow Arab Americans with the idea that supporting the hospital would be a noble way to honor their immigrant forefathers. The ALSAC was founded in 1957 and has assumed full responsibility for the hospital's fund-raising efforts. Headquartered in Memphis, Tennessee, the organization is America's fourth largest not-for-profit health-related fund-raising organization and is supported by more than one million volunteers nationwide.

Did You Know? This Arab American of Lebanese descent helped develop the artificial heart and was the first surgeon to successfully use a heart pump in a patient. Who is he? *(answer on following page)*

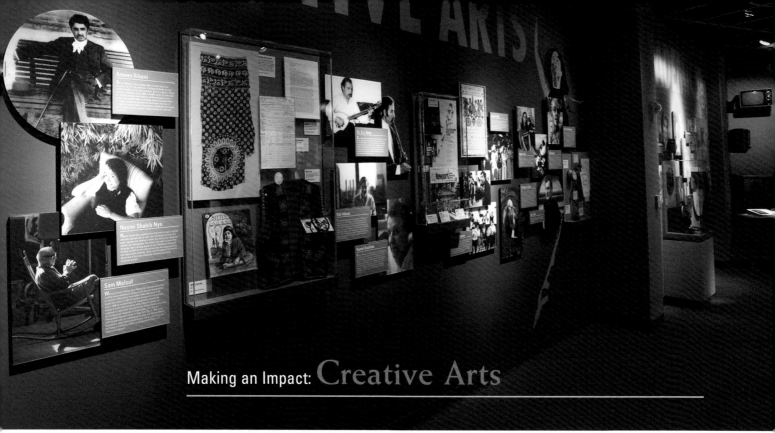

Making an Impact: Creative Arts

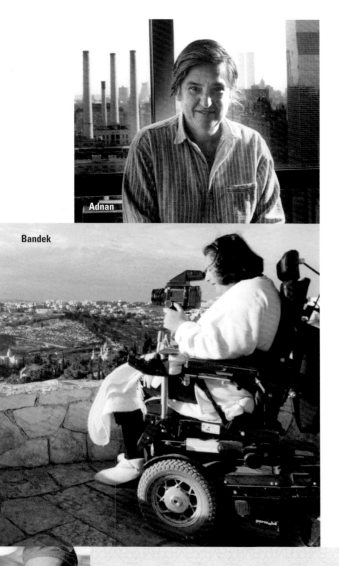

Adnan

Bandek

Etel Adnan

Internationally acclaimed artist and writer Etel Adnan is the author of more than ten books of poetry and literature. Her novel on the Lebanese civil war, *Sitt Marie Rose*, has been translated into more than ten languages. Explaining her visual artwork, she wrote, "Abstract art was the equivalent of poetic expression; I didn't need to use words, but colors and lines. I didn't need to belong to a language-oriented culture but to an open form of expression." Adnan has studied in Lebanon, France, and in the United States.

Lily Bandek

The first Arab American photographer to have her work accepted in the permanent collection of the White House, Lily Bandek was the personal photographer of Mrs. Anwar Sadat and King Hussein and Queen Noor of Jordan. After being diagnosed with multiple sclerosis in 1984, she designed a camera that could be mounted on a wheelchair so that she could continue working. In 1994, she established the Bandek Foundation, which encourages people with disabilities to enter the workforce. Born in Amman, Jordan, Bandek has lived in the United States since 1960.

Answer: Michael Debakey: surgeon, inventor, political advisor, medical consultant.

Naomi Shihab Nye

Shortly after she learned how to write, Naomi published her first poem at age seven. Her continued success as a poet, essayist, and children's book writer has earned her numerous awards and fellowships. Author and editor of more than twenty works, Nye's writing draws on her Palestinian American heritage as well as the cultural diversity she experiences in her home of San Antonio, Texas and throughout her travels. She is one of the most influential contemporary Arab American writers.

Nye

Kamal Boullata

Kamal Boullata is a Palestinian American artist from Jerusalem whose work often reflects the visual landscape of his childhood. His work is found in collections around the world, including Morocco, France, and the United States. After studying art in Rome and Washington, D.C., he opened Alif Gallery, which is the first gallery dedicated to contemporary Arab art, in Washington, D.C. An active supporter of the Palestinian cause, he is a prolific writer and has published numerous scholarly articles and books on contemporary Palestinian and Arab art, as well as a children's book on Palestine.

Boullata

Elie Chaib

Both the youngest and oldest dancer for the legendary Paul Taylor Company in New York City, Elie Chaib has been dancing for the company for an unprecedented twenty seasons. He was named Dancer of the Year in 1992 by the New York Times.

Chaib

Ghada Amer

Ghada Amer has received numerous awards from the international arts community, including the UNESCO Award at the 1999 Venice Biennale. Her work challenges gender stereotypes and redefines the relationship between East and West, male and female, art and craft. Born in Cairo, Amer was trained in Paris and now lives and works in New York City.

Amer

El-Dabh

Rihani

Shaheen, child in middle front playing the Oud

Dr. Halim El-Dabh

Born in 1921, Halim El-Dabh is considered one of the most accomplished living composers of our time. His music has been internationally celebrated, particularly in his birthplace of Egypt, where his compositions are heard in the *Sound and Light of the Pyramids of Giza*, which is performed regularly at the Pyramids. He has received numerous awards, including two Rockefeller fellowships, two Guggenheim fellowships, and two Fulbright fellowships. In 1969, he took a teaching position at Kent State University, where he unofficially retired in 1991, yet remains an adjunct professor in the Department of Pan-African Studies.

Ameen Rihani

Ameen Rihani is the founding father of Arab American literature. In 1911, he published *The Book of Khalid*, the first novel in English by an Arab American. Born in Lebanon, he moved to New York City in 1888. Rihani was a prolific writer who published his articles, essays, short stories, novels, and poetry both in Arabic and English. His writings explore the possibilities of cultural exchange between the Arab world and the United States. In 2002, the Ameen Rihani Organization established the Ameen Rihani Scholarship to provide college funding for Lebanese Americans.

Simon Shaheen

Infusing traditional Arabic music with jazz and classical styles, Simon Shaheen has earned international acclaim as a virtuoso on the oud and violin. His unique contributions were recognized in 1994 when he received the celebrated National Heritage Award from the National Endowment for the Arts. Born in Jerusalem, Palestine, he currently lives in New York City, where he formed the Near Eastern Music Ensemble in the 1980s.

Dr. A. J. Racy

One of the world's foremost experts on traditional Arab music, A. J. Racy is an accomplished performer, composer, and ethnomusicologist. He is a master musician who plays many instruments, including the oud, the rabbabah, and the mijwiz. Born in Lebanon, he teaches at the University of California in Los Angeles. Through his performances and teaching, Racy has brought traditional Arab music to Arab Americans and American culture.

Gibran Khalil Gibran

Gibran Khalil Gibran came to Boston's South End from
the small village of Bsharri in Lebanon in 1895. Like
Ameen Rihani, he wrote in both Arabic and English.
He published his first article in 1904 in the Arab
American newspaper, *Al-Mouhajer (The Emigrant)*.
He was actively involved in literary circles and founded
the Pen League in 1911 with fellow Arab American
writer Mikhail Naimy. His world-renowned reputation
came with the 1923 publication of *The Prophet*, which
has been translated into more than twenty languages.
A celebrated novelist and poet, he was also an accomplished painter.

Gibran

Sam Maloof

Without formal training, Sam Maloof has become
one of the world's most celebrated craftsmen and the
only woodworker and furniture designer to receive a
MacArthur Foundation Fellowship Award. He began his
career in 1934 by building furniture for his parents and
in 1948 he received his first commission. Uniting the
beauty of craft with functional utility, his works are
exhibited in collections throughout the United States,
including the Smithsonian Institution in Washington,
D.C. and the Metropolitan Museum of Art in New York
City. In 1994, along with his late wife, Alfreda, he established the Sam and Alfreda Maloof Foundation, dedicated to fostering the role of craft in society. His home in
California, which he designed and built, is a historical landmark that is open to the public.

Maloof

Low-back chair made by Sam
Maloof especially for the Arab
American National Museum

Hamza El Din

The father of modern Nubian music,
Hamza El Din performs throughout
the world. After graduating with a
degree in electrical engineering, he
taught himself the oud and the tar
(a traditional Nubian instrument). He
has since become one of the world's
most prominent musicians. El Din
was born in the Sudan, and he
currently resides in San Francisco.

Playing with the Grateful Dead, Hamza
El Din is front row, fifth from the right

Making an Impact: Academics

Adamany

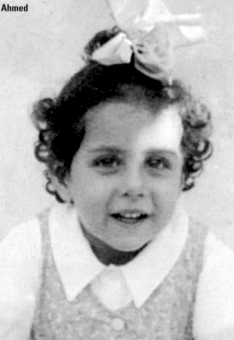

Ahmed

Dr. David Adamany

The eighth and longest-serving president of Detroit's Wayne State University, Dr. David Adamany served from 1982 to 1997. During this time, he reorganized the university and created three new colleges: The School of Fine and Performing Arts, the College of Urban, Labor and Metropolitan Affairs in 1985, and the College of Science in 1993. He also launched the largest building program in Wayne State's history. Today, he is president of Temple University in Pittsburgh.

Dr. Leila Ahmed

In 1999, Leila Ahmed became the first professor of Women's Studies in Religion at Harvard Divinity School. Born in Cairo, Egypt in 1940, she received her Ph.D. from Cambridge University. A leading scholar on gender and Islam, her works include *Women and Gender in Islam: Historical Roots of a Modern Debate* (1992) and *A Border Passage: From Cairo to America—A Woman's Journey* (1999).

Mulhair being named Acalanes Union High School District's Teacher of the Year in 1994

Mona Salem Mulhair

Born in Egypt, Mona Salem Mulhair graduated first in her class from Cairo's Ain Shams University. She came to the United States in the early 1980s and received a Master's degree in French Language and Literature from Middlebury College. She has served as a reader and consultant for the College Board French Exam since 1995. She is credited for establishing the first French AP Program at Cairo American College.

Dr. Philip Hitti

In 1947, Dr. Philip Hitti established the Near Eastern Studies program at Princeton University, the first such program in the United States. He came to the United States from Lebanon in 1913 and three years later received his Ph.D. from Columbia University. During the ninety-two years of his life, he established himself as a preeminent scholar of Arab history. His book, *History of the Arabs*, first published in 1937, remains the standard work in the field and has been printed in eleven editions.

Mona Mulhair in her Cairo, Egypt home at a reception for President Mohamed Najeeb. She is being greeted by then Minister of Agriculture, Abdel Aziz Abdallah Salem.

Dr. Hitti, center

Did You Know? Writer, director, and producer William Peter Blatty won an Academy Award for the screenplay of a famous horror film, which he adapted from his original novel of the same name. What was the film? *(answer on following page)*

161

Dr. Alixa Naff and her assistant organizing data she brought back from the field, circa 1980.

Dr. Alixa Naff

After earning a degree in history from the University of California at Los Angeles, Dr. Alixa Naff set off on a trip that would spark a lifelong devotion to collecting and preserving the stories of Arab immigrants who came to the United States. Armed with a tape recorder and a $1000 grant from the UCLA Folklore Department, she spent the summer of 1962 collecting oral histories throughout North America. In 1984, she donated her artifacts, photographs, and oral histories to the American History Museum of the Smithsonian, establishing the first Arab American collection in the nation, the Naff Collection.

Dr. Jack Shaheen

Dr. Jack Shaheen has dedicated his life to exposing stereotypes of Arabs and Arab Americans in Hollywood. He is an internationally acclaimed author and media critic. A former CBS News consultant on Middle East affairs and Professor Emeritus of Mass Communications at Southern Illinois University, he has written several books, including *Reel Bad Arabs: How Hollywood Vilifies a People, Arab and Muslim Stereotyping in American Popular Culture, Nuclear War Films,* and *The Arab TV.*

Shaheen

In Memoriam
Edward W. Said
Readings and Music

Said's glasses

Dr. Edward Said

Dr. Edward Said was one of the most distinguished intellectuals of the twentieth century. His 1978 book, *Orientalism,* is credited with launching the field of Post-Colonial studies in Comparative Literature. In *Orientalism,* he proposes new ways of examining how the Arab world is represented in Europe and America. Born in Jerusalem in 1935, he was one of the most influential voices for the Palestinian cause in the United States and England. In addition to his work as an academic, essayist, and public lecturer, Said was an accomplished pianist and opera critic.

Dr. Salah Hassan

Hassan

Dr. Salah Hassan is one of the first art historians and critics in the field of contemporary African and Arab art. Under his direction, the Forum for African Arts, a nonprofit organization, maintains the presence of contemporary African arts on a global scale. He co-curated an unprecedented exhibit of contemporary African arts at the 2001 Venice Biennale entitled *Authentic/Ex-Centric: Africa In and Out of Africa.* He grew up in the Sudan and is the Chair of the Department of the History of Art at Cornell University. He also is one of the founding editors of *Nka: Journal of Contemporary African Art.*

Answer: *The Exorcist*

Politics

John Sununu

This former New Hampshire governor and White House Chief of Staff spent six years as a cohost of CNN's political debate show, *Crossfire*. Born in Cuba to a family of Palestinian-Lebanese ancestry, Sununu became New Hampshire's governor in 1983. After serving three consecutive terms, Ronald Reagan commissioned him as Chief of Staff in 1989. Former Governor Sununu served in the George H. W. Bush White House until 1992, when he became the national co-chairman of the Bush/Quayle campaign.

Victor Atiyeh

In 1981, the U.S. Department of Justice awarded former Oregon Governor, Victor Atiyeh, the highest public service honor for his dedication to passing laws against racial harassment. Before entering the political realm, he began his career at a Portland rug and carpet firm established by his father and uncle. From 1959 to 1964 he served as a member of the Oregon House of Representatives. The former governor also served as state senator from 1965 to 1978, acting for three legislative sessions as Senate Republican leader. In 1978, he was elected Governor for the State of Oregon.

John Sununu with President George H. W. Bush in 1990.

Atiyeh

Did You Know? This Arab American's writings inspired President John F. Kennedy's famous "Ask not what your country can do for you — ask what you can do for your country" speech. Who is he? *(answer on following page)*

163

Mitchell

George Mitchell

Former Senate Majority Leader George Mitchell brokered a peace agreement in Northern Ireland, which won him a number of awards, including the Presidential Medal of Freedom, which is the highest civilian honor the U.S. government can award; the Philadelphia Liberty Medal; the Truman Institute Peace Prize; and the United Nations (UNESCO) Peace Prize. In 1977, he became U.S. Attorney for the State of Maine and in 1979 President Jimmy Carter appointed him U.S. District Court Judge. Twice he was elected to the Senate, in 1982 and 1988. As a senator, he served on several committees, chairing the Democratic Senatorial Campaign Committee and acting as a member of the Select Committee on the Iran-Contra Affair. He pushed legislation on several fronts, most successfully with environmental and health care acts.

James Abdnor

James Abdnor began his political career in South Dakota, where he served in the Senate from 1956 to 1968. Following that, he became President of the Senate and South Dakota's Lieutenant Governor. In 1973, he was elected to the U.S. House of Representatives. He went on to serve in the U.S. Senate and then the Small Business Administration. House Resolution No. 1001, adopted on February 18, 2003, honored Abdnor on his eightieth birthday.

Abdnor

Helen Thomas

Cited by the World Almanac as one of the 25 Most Influential Women in America, Helen Thomas earned the title "First Lady of the Press" for her role as Dean of the White House Press Corps and her work as White House Bureau Chief. For fifty-seven years, she served as White House correspondent for United Press International, covering every United States president since John F. Kennedy. She was the only female print journalist to travel with President Richard Nixon during his trip to China in January 1972. Since then, she has traveled the world with Presidents Nixon, Ford, Carter, Reagan, George H. W. Bush, Clinton, and George W. Bush.

Thomas and portable typewriter carried early in her career

Answer: Kahlil Gibran—poet, artist. Gibran's words are: "Are you a politician asking what your country can do for you or a zealous one asking what you can do for your country?"

Nick Joe Rahall II

Since 1976, West Virginia Congressman Nick Joe Rahall II has served more than a dozen terms representing his state's Third Congressional District, a post to which he was elected in 1976. He has served on the House Committee on Resources as the ranking Democratic member and on the Committee on Transportation and Infrastructure as the second senior Democrat. A leader in mining-related issues, he served eight years as chair of the House Subcommittee on Mining and Natural Resources. In 1993, he became chairman of the House Surface Transportation Committee.

John Baldacci

John Baldacci became Governor of Maine in 2002 and has been recognized for his accomplishments by the National Energy Assistance Directors Association; the Congressional Youth Leadership Council; NASA; the Maine State Society of Washington, D.C.; and the American Humane Association. His political career began in 1982 when he won a seat in the Maine Senate. In 1994, he was elected to represent Maine's Second District in the U.S. House of Representatives. Reelected three times, he served on the House Agricultural Committee and the Committee on Transportation and Infrastructure.

Mary Rose Oakar

Mary Rose Oakar became the president of the American-Arab Anti-Discrimination Committee in 2003. She was named one of the "Ten Best Legislators in Congress" by *50 Plus Magazine* and one of the "Ten Best Members of Congress for Health and Women's Issues" by *McCall's* Magazine. From the Cleveland City Council, she went on to represent Ohio's Twentieth District as a Democratic congresswoman from 1977 to 1993. In 2000, she began a three-year term with the Ohio House of Representatives. She received several awards, including the American Cancer Society's Distinguished Service Award for Legislation, the Consumer Federation of America's Legislator of the Year Award, and the National Association for Homecare's Award for Working on Aging Issues.

Rahall

Baldacci

Oakar

Did You Know? This person was America's first Jet Ace and a Triple Ace in the Korean War. For his accomplishments, an airport in Wichita, Kansas has been named after him. Who is he? *(answer on following page)*

165

Abourezk

Barkett

Daniels

James Abourezk

James Abourezk is the founder of the American-Arab Anti-Discrimination Committee. Raised by Lebanese immigrants on a Sioux Indian reservation in South Dakota, he served in the U.S. House of Representatives from 1971 to 1973 and in the U.S. Senate from 1973 to 1979. He is a staunch supporter of environmental concerns, Native American rights, and a more evenhanded U.S. policy on the Arab-Israeli conflict. His public interest work includes acting as voluntary chief legal officer for the Navajo Indians of Arizona and New Mexico.

Rosemary Barkett

Rosemary Barkett was the first woman to serve on Florida's Supreme Court. A former nun, she was born to Syrian parents in a small town in Mexico. In 1979, she served as a Circuit Judge in Palm Beach County. Appointed to Florida's Fourth District Court of Appeals in 1984, she was appointed to the Supreme Court of Florida a year later. She has served as the Court's Chief Justice since 1992 and was appointed by President Clinton to the U.S. Court of Appeals for the Eleventh Circuit in 1993. She has been inducted into the Florida Women's Hall of Fame.

Mitchell Daniels, Jr.

In the early 1980s, Mitchell Daniels, Jr. served as Executive Director of the National Republican Senatorial Committee. He began work in 2001 as President George W. Bush's Director of the Office of Management and Budget (OMB) from January 2001 through June 2003. In this role he was also a member of the National Security Council and the Homeland Security Council. On January 5, 2005 he began his four-year term as Governor of Indiana.

Answer: Colonel James Jabara: American Jet Ace and namesake of the Col. James Jabara Airport in Wichita, Kansas.

Darrell Issa

Darrell Issa is an entrepreneur-turned-congressman who co-chaired the campaign to pass the California Civil Rights Initiative and was a driving force behind the recall of California Governor Gray Davis. First elected to Congress in 2000, he has served on the House International Relations Committee, Judiciary Committee, and Small Business Committee. He also served as Vice Chairman of the House Republican Policy Subcommittee on Biotechnology, Telecommunications and Information Technology. Before entering politics, he founded Directed Electronics, an automobile security systems manufacturing company, and in 1994, he received Inc. Magazine's Entrepreneur of the Year Award. He also serves on the House Government Reform Committee where he is Chairman of the Subcommittee on Energy and Resources.

Chris John

Chris John, born on January 5, 1960, is a leading advocate for environmental issues and farmers' rights. As a Democratic Congressman representing Louisiana's Seventh Congressional District from 1997 to 2005, he served on the House Energy and Commerce Committee, where his efforts included creating a national energy policy. He also has been a member of the Energy and Air Quality and Health subcommittees.

Ray LaHood

Congressman Ray LaHood is a staunch supporter of civil causes and environmental issues. As a representative of Illinois's Eighteenth Congressional District, he has served as Chairman of the Terrorism and Homeland Security Subcommittee and Vice Chairman of the Intelligence Policy and National Security Subcommittee. In addition, he has served on the House Appropriations Committee and the House Permanent Select Committee on Intelligence. He has twice attended Alabama's Civil Rights Pilgrimage and also works to preserve the Illinois River.

Issa making a speech

John

LaHood

Isaac

Zogby (right)

Selwa Roosevelt (left) with
President Ronald Reagan,
December 15, 1983.

Teresa Isaac

Teresa Isaac is a second-generation Arab American born and raised in Kentucky. She is the longest serving vice mayor of Lexington, Kentucky, holding that position from 1993 to 1999. She was elected mayor of Lexington in 2002. Prior to entering a career in public service, she was a prosecutor and associate professor. During her years as an attorney, Mayor Isaac was credited with bringing equity into Kentucky sports. For those efforts she received a National Sports Equity Commendation and the Golden Gazelle Award in 1988.

John Zogby

As president and CEO of the public opinion research and polling company Zogby International, John Zogby provides valuable statistical information to politicians, journalists, and policymakers. He works as a pollster for various news agencies, including Reuters, NBC News, MSNBC, *The New York Post*, and Fox News. He appears frequently on television shows, such as NBC's *Today Show* and ABC's *Good Morning America*. He has taught history and political science at the State University of New York, Utica College, and Hamilton College's Arthur Levitt Public Affairs Center. He also is Senior Associate of Global Affairs of Citizenship and Public Affairs at Syracuse University's Maxwell School.

Selwa Roosevelt

Selwa Roosevelt served as Chief of Protocol for the United States from 1982 to 1989 and was nominated to the rank of Ambassador. Before working at the White House, she worked for *The Washington Post* and free-lanced for various magazines. The wife of Archibald B. Roosevelt, President Theodore Roosevelt's grandson, she was awarded the Outstanding Civilian Service Medal by the Department of the Army and given the Ripon Society's Salute to Republican Women award. In 1990, she published her autobiography, *Keeper of the Gate*.

Donna Shalala

Donna Shalala, daughter of Lebanese parents, served
as the U.S. Secretary of Health and Human Services
under President Bill Clinton and is the first woman to
head a Big Ten school. Her public service record
includes chairing the Children's Defense Fund and
working as Assistant Secretary for policy research and
development at the Department of Housing and Urban
Development. In 1988, she was appointed Chancellor
of the University of Wisconsin-Madison and in 2001
she became President of the University of Miami. She
received more than three dozen honorary degrees as
well as honors that include the National Public Service
Award and a Guggenheim fellowship.

Spencer Abraham

In 2001, Spencer Abraham became the U.S. Secretary
of Energy under President George W. Bush. Before
that, he served six years as a U.S. Senator from
Michigan. His other political achievements include
serving as co-chairman of the National Republican
Congressional Committee, chairing the Michigan
Republican Party, and acting as Deputy Chief of Staff
to former Vice President Dan Quayle.

James Zogby

James Zogby is the President of the Arab American
Institute, an organization he established in Washington
D.C. in 1985 to enhance Arab American political
empowerment through voter registration, education,
and mobilization. A cofounder and chairman of the
Palestine Human Rights Campaign in the late 1970s,
he later served as the Director of the American-Arab
Anti-Discrimination Committee. In 1982, he cofounded
Save Lebanon, a humanitarian relief agency that funds
Palestinian and Lebanese organizations that provide
aid to victims of war. He is an active member of the
Democratic Party.

Shalala with children

Abraham

James Zogby with Senator Ted Kennedy

Did You Know? Arab American Robert George worked at the White House for fifty years serving under seven administrations.
What was his job? *(answer on following page)*

Making an Impact: Sports

Doug Flutie

Darren Flutie

Doug Flutie

Football player Doug Flutie has achieved a number of "firsts" in his career, starting with his days as an All American quarterback at Boston College. His 48-yard, no-time-left touchdown pass that gave Boston a 47-45 victory over the 1983 National Champion Miami Hurricanes ranks as one of the most thrilling plays in college football history. He won the 1984 Heisman Trophy, setting the all-time major college career passing record (10,579 yards) and the all-time major college career total offense record (11,054 yards). He went on to play for the Chicago Bears, the New England Patriots, the Buffalo Bills, and the San Diego Chargers. During his time away from the NFL, he played for eight years in the Canadian Football League, winning the Grey Cup Most Outstanding Player award an unprecedented six times. In honor of his son, who has autism, Flutie established the Doug Flutie Jr. Foundation for Autism, Inc. in 2000.

Darren Flutie

Darren Flutie played for the San Diego Chargers of the National Football League. He was drafted by the Canadian Football League and as a wide receiver he reigns as the CFL's current leader in all-time catches. He retired from the CFL in 2003 as career leader in season and playoff receptions (972 season receptions, 85 playoff receptions). He is also tied with Allen Pitts for the most seasons with at least 1,000 yards receiving. He played in four Grey Cup games, winning two of them.

Answer: Robert George was the official White House Santa Claus.

Joe LaHoud, Jr.

Joe LaHoud, Jr. is known to fans and teammates as "Duck." He signed with the Boston Red Sox in 1966 as an amateur free agent. He went on to play for the Milwaukee Brewers, the California Angels, the Texas Rangers, and the Kansas City Royals. In 1978, he ended his career with 65 home runs and 218 RBIs in 791 games.

Fred Saigh

Fred Saigh modernized the baseball business by creating an affordable ticket system for the World Series. He grew up in Illinois, helping his parents run their chain of grocery stores. A successful corporate and tax law attorney, he purchased the St. Louis Cardinals and became sole owner in 1949. Adamant that the Cardinals stay in St. Louis, he sold the team in 1953 to Anheuser-Busch for just $750,000. Paying a waitress' college tuition and helping a maintenance man pay his mother's mortgage are only two of many stories that exemplify his generosity. His legacy continues through the Saigh Foundation that supports charitable organizations in the St. Louis metropolitan region. Saigh died in 1999 at the age of ninety-four.

Drew Haddad

As a wide receiver for the University of Buffalo, Drew Haddad was the school's all-time leading receiver and held twelve different records. After graduation, he was drafted by the National Football League's Buffalo Bills and then went on to play for the Indianapolis Colts. He currently plays for the World League's Frankfurt Galaxy.

Bill George

Elected to the Pro Football Hall of Fame in 1974, Bill George was the first Arab American to play football's middle linebacker position and is considered one of the best in the sport's history. He played with the Chicago Bears, and his fifteen-year career boasts eight Pro-Bowl selections and a 1963 Western Conference championship. He established the Bill George Youth Football League more than thirty years ago for young players in the suburban Chicago area.

LaHoud

Saigh

Haddad

George

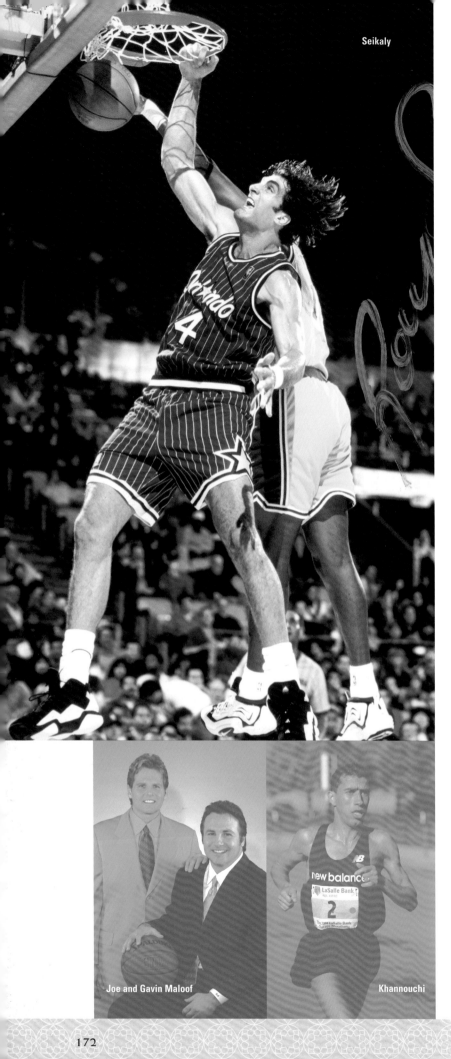

Seikaly

Joe and Gavin Maloof

Khannouchi

Rony Seikaly

Star basketball player Rony Seikaly ranked as Syracuse University's all-time leading scorer until his record was broken by Derrick Coleman. In the 1988 National Basketball Association draft, he was selected in the first round by the Miami Heat. Born in 1965 in Beirut, he attended high school at the American School in Athens, Greece. Every year, he hosts the Rony Seikaly Golf Tournament to benefit cystic fibrosis.

Joe and Gavin Maloof

Joe and Gavin Maloof, owners of Maloof Sports and Entertainment, preside over a business that stretches across California, Nevada, Colorado, and New Mexico. In 1999, the brothers bought the National Basketball Association's Sacramento Kings, the Women's National Basketball Association's Sacramento Monarchs, and Sacramento's ARCO Arena. The Maloof family annually donates more than $1 million to charitable causes and in 2001, the brothers were given the Sports Humanitarian World Hall of Fame's Most Involved Executives award.

Khalid Khannouchi

Khalid Khannouchi is a world-class marathon runner. Born in 1971 in Meknes, Morocco, he is 5'5" tall and weighs 125 pounds. His recent marathon records include a 2:05:42 finish in 1999 in Chicago and a 2:05:38 finish in London in 2002.

The Sheik

The Sheik

Ed Farhat, more famously known as the Sheik, revolutionized professional wrestling with his unorthodox inclusion of fire throwing, barbed wire, and an assortment of other foreign objects. Beginning his career in 1951, he wrestled until the 1990s, when he was nearly seventy. With Detroit as a base, his *Big Time Wrestling* television show and live events were a major part of the National Wrestling Alliance. He died in 2003 at age seventy-eight.

Michael Adray

The best friend of sports in Michigan, Michael Adray sponsored his first amateur baseball team in 1956 and continued on to sponsor hockey, softball, soccer, basketball, and wrestling programs. For many years, he provided over fifteen thousand youth and adults with the uniforms needed to play, which led mothers all over the state to repeatedly tell him that their children were sleeping in the shirts he generously provided. His contributions offer continued proof of the importance of youth athletics; seventy Adray Collegiate Baseball League alumni who have played in the Majors include Orel Hershiser, Frank Tanana, Jim Abbott, and Barry Larkin.

Mike Adray (left) and Joe Hallissey greet attendees at a dinner recognizing Adray, October 1991.

Bobby Rahal

In the world of automobile racing, Bobby Rahal has reached the highest levels. The Indianapolis 500 Winner and three-time CART Series Champion went from a childhood racing sports cars with his father to a career competing in racing's elite: Formula 1 and Indycars. In 1996, he partnered with talk show host David Letterman to establish Team Rahal. He continued driving Indycars until 1998, when he retired to concentrate on running his team and developing automobile dealerships in Pennsylvania and Ohio. After a stint in Europe as Chief Executive of Jaguar's Formula 1 Racing Operations, he returned to the United States, where he runs a variety of racing teams and drives in historic races.

Rahal

MEADOWLANDS INDY

The New York Times

SPORTS

Section 5

Sunday, June 1, 1986

Special: Westchester/Connecticut Automobile Exchange   C/W

Rahal Wins Indy 500 in Closest Three-Car Finish

Cogan Is 2d And Mears 3d

By FRANK LITSKY

Making an Impact: Entertainers

Abraham with Best Actor Academy Award (below) and Best Supporting Actor Golden Globe Award (left)

Akkad

PAUL ANKA/LONELY BOY

LONELY BOY
AUTUMN LEAVES
LES FILLES DE PARIS
FAR FROM THE LIGHTS OF TOWN   IT ONLY LASTS F

VOCAL   PAUL ANKA
"my WAY"

Paula Abdul

You've seen her on TV's *American Idol*. You've heard her on the radio. And you've seen her dance moves performed by superstars like Janet Jackson. She is Paula Abdul: dancer, choreographer, and pop singer. She began her career as a Los Angeles Lakers cheerleader. In 1988, her debut album, *Forever Your Girl*, sold more than ten million copies and included four No.1 singles: "Straight Up," "Cold Hearted," "Opposites Attract," and "Forever Your Girl." Her 1991 follow-up album, *Spellbound*, went multi-platinum. It produced the No.1 singles "Rush, Rush" and "The Promise of a New Day."

F. Murray Abraham

F. Murray Abraham is an Academy Award winner who took home Best Actor for portraying the tormented musician, Salieri, in the movie, *Amadeus*. He has appeared in numerous other films, including *Mighty Aphrodite*, *Finding Forrester*, and *Falcone*. And did you know that he once worked as Santa at a Macy's department store?

Moustapha Akkad

Producer and director Moustapha Akkad's film credits include *The Lion in the Desert* and *The Message*. In 2002, he served as Executive Producer of *Halloween: Resurrection*. Born in Aleppo, Syria, he is the founder of Akkad International Productions, Inc. In 1978, he formed Filmco Executive Productions. In November 2005, Akkad died as a result of injuries sustained from the bombing of the hotel in which he was staying in Jordan.

Paul Anka

When Paul Anka appeared at age sixteen on *American Bandstand* to sing his first No.1 hit, "Diana," he became one of America's first teen pop idols. Since then, he has written music for the world's best-known performers, including "My Way" for Frank Sinatra and the theme music for the *Tonight Show* with Johnny Carson. His other top ten songs include: "You Are My Destiny," "Lonely Boy," "Put Your Head on My Shoulder," "It's Time to Cry," "Puppy Love," and "My Home Town." In 1978, he was honored with a star on Hollywood's Walk of Fame.

Michael Ansara

Michael Ansara rose to fame in the 1950s playing Cochise on *Broken Arrow,* a popular TV western. Born in Syria, he immigrated to the United States at the age of two. He went on to act in more than sixty Hollywood films, including *The Ten Commandments* and *The Lone Ranger.* He has also appeared as a guest on more than fifty-five television shows, including *Murder She Wrote, Gunsmoke, The Fugitive, The Untouchables, Fantasy Island, Star Trek: Voyager, I Dream of Jeannie,* and *The Rockford Files.*

Don Bustany

This radio and television pioneer cocreated *American Top 40* and *American Country Countdown with Casey Kasem.* After completing his service for the Korean Conflict in 1954, he left his Ph.D. work at Wayne State University and went to Los Angeles to find fame and fortune. In the late 1960s he met Casey Kasem and the two decided to work on a project together. Their first broadcast of *American Top 40* was aired July 4, 1970. He also worked in television as director of the 1970s sitcom, *The Bob Newhart Show.*

Dick Dale

Known as the king of the surf guitar, Dick Dale invented the loud, staccato style of music in the 1960s with his band, The Deltones, the first surf rock group. He was the first rock guitarist to perform on the *Ed Sullivan Show* and was inducted into the Surfing Hall of Fame and the Hollywood Rock Walk of Fame. Today, you can hear his music at Disney's Magic Mountain and in the film *Pulp Fiction.* His song "Miserlou" heads up the platinum-selling soundtrack.

George Dibie

George Dibie is a six-time Emmy Award-winning cinematographer whose TV credits include shows such as *Barney Miller, Murphy Brown, Night Court, Growing Pains,* and *Mr. Belvedere.* Born and raised in Jerusalem, he studied at the Pasadena Playhouse College of Theatre Arts. He had his first big break supervising camera work on the *Barney Miller* show. In 1985, he became the first National President of the International Cinematographer Guild. He is also the first individual inducted into the Showbiz Expo Hall of Fame.

Ansara

Bustany as a child (front)

Dibie

Dibie's light meter

Did You Know? He is considered one of the most original and complex figures in rock culture. He rose to fame in the early 1960s, leading a group called Mothers of Invention and has released more than fifty albums. Who is he? *(answer on following page)*

Actor Jaime Farr is best known for his role as Corporal Maxwell Klinger from the television show, *M*A*S*H*. This fatigue-covered script (right) is from the last episode of the critically-acclaimed series entitled, "Goodbye, Farewell, Amen."

Shannon Elizabeth

This young actress grew up in Texas. Before beginning her acting career, she traveled around the world as a model. She can be seen in numerous movies and TV shows, most notably the *American Pie* trilogy, *Scary Movie*, and *Jay and Silent Bob Strike Back*.

Jamie Farr

For eleven years, Jamie Farr was known to fans of the hit TV show *M*A*S*H* as Corporal Maxwell Klinger. This popular actor studied acting at the Pasadena Playhouse and has been working since 1955, when he scored his first film role in *The Blackboard Jungle*. His recent projects include the 2004 film, *Cyber Meltdown*. Born in Toledo, Ohio, Farr sometimes goes by the name Jameel. He believes strongly in giving back to his community; in 2003, the Jamie Farr Owens Corning Classic golf tournament raised $580,000 for Ohio charities. He has hosted the women's professional golf event since 1984.

Salma Hayek

A critically acclaimed actress and spokesmodel for Revlon cosmetics, Salma Hayek is the star of such films as *Wild Wild West, Traffic, Dogma, 54,* and *Fools Rush In*. Born in 1966 in Mexico to a Lebanese father and Mexican mother, she began her career in television before getting her big break in the film, *Desperado*. In 2003, she was nominated for an Academy Award and a Golden Globe for her title role in the film, *Frieda*, which she also produced.

Asaad Kelada

Born in Cairo, Egypt, Asaad Kelada has directed many popular television shows, such as *Everybody Loves Raymond, Dharma and Greg, The Facts of Life, Who's the Boss?, WKRP in Cincinnati, Designing Women, Married People, Family Ties,* and *Sister, Sister*.

Callie Khouri

Callie Khouri won an Oscar for Best Original Screenplay for her work on the film, *Thelma and Louise*, which she also coproduced. Her other screenplay projects include *Something to Talk About* and *The Divine Secrets of the YaYa Sisterhood*, which she also directed.

Kelada

Answer: Frank Zappa: bandleader, guitarist, composer, satirist, and political commentator.

Herbert Khaury

Herbert Khaury, aka Tiny Tim, was a ukulele-playing pop singer beloved for his high voice, childlike stage persona, and flair for self-promotion. Tiny Tim got his stage name from an agent who worked with little people, and he built an entire career around his hit song, "Tiptoe Thru the Tulips." His 1969 marriage to Vicki Budinger on Johnny Carson's *Tonight Show* attracted 40 million viewers. After his death in 1996, Carson told TV Guide, "He was one of the most ingenuous persons I have ever known."

Khaury

Emile Kuri

The acclaimed art director and set decorator Emile Kuri has received eight Academy Award nominations for films such as *Bedknobs and Broomsticks, The Absent-Minded Professor, Carrie, Executive Suite, Mary Poppins,* and *Silver Queen.* He won Oscars in Art Direction for *The Heiress* and for *20,000 Leagues Under the Sea.*

Wendie Malick

An actress and a community activist, Wendie Malick's career has transitioned from modeling to award-winning television and screen roles. She received both Golden Globe and Emmy nominations for playing Nina Van Horn on TV's *Just Shoot Me.* Before that, she won four Cable ACE Awards for her starring role in HBO's *Dream On.* She is involved with numerous community projects, including Planned Parenthood, Adopt-A-Family, domestic violence prevention, and environmental advocacy. In 1995, she helped create The Maverick Building Squad, a nonprofit organization that builds houses in underdeveloped areas of Mexico.

Malick

Michelle Nader

Television writer Michelle Nader has had a hand in penning some of TV's best-loved shows such as *The King of Queens, Dharma and Greg, Spin City,* and *Caroline in the City.*

Steven Naifeh

An author and publisher, Steven Naifeh won the Pulitzer Prize for his biography of the artist Jackson Pollack. His book, *Jackson Pollack: An American Saga,* was later adapted into an Academy Award-winning film.

Najimy

Noujaim

Rehm

Kathy Najimy

You know this actress's face from TV shows such as *Veronica's Closet* and films such as *Sister Act*. If you're a *King of the Hill* fan, then you know her voice, too; she portrays Peggy Hill on the Emmy Award-winning animated series. As an actress, Kathy Najimy has appeared in numerous films, including *Hocus Pocus, Hope Floats, The Fisher King, Soapdish,* and HBO's *If These Walls Could Talk*. She has won numerous awards for her work on both the screen and the stage. Also an activist, she has been honored with the L.A. Shanti's Founder Award and the L.A. Gay and Lesbian Center's Distinguished Achievement Award. For her dedication to animal rights, she received the Humanitarian of the Year award from People for the Ethical Treatment of Animals.

Jehane Noujaim

When it comes to making films, Jehane Noujaim seems to do it all. For her 2001 debut, *Startup.com*, she acted as director, cinematographer, producer, and executive producer. She grew up in Cairo and has also directed several documentaries in the Arab world. After graduating from Harvard University with high distinction, she went to work for MTV until 1995 when she started her own company, Noujaim Films. In 1999, she joined Pennebaker Hegedus Films.

Michael Nouri

Actor Michael Nouri can be seen on the stage, film screen, and television. He starred in the television and Broadway versions of *Victor/Victoria*. He also starred in the films *Flashdance* and *Finding Forrester* and the TV comedy series *Love and War*.

Diane Rehm

The daughter to an Egyptian mother, Diane Rehm is a writer, radio producer, talk show host, and is best known for her work on National Public Radio's *The Diane Rehm Show*. Over the years, she received many honors, including the International Matrix Award from Women in Communications. The Society of Professional Journalists has honored her as a Fellow, the highest honor the society can bestow.

Fred Saidy

Playwright Fred Saidy has written the script for several Broadway shows such as *The Bloomer Girl, Finian's Rainbow, Flahooley, Jamaica,* and *The Happiest Girl* in the World.

Ronald Schwary

Ronald Schwary produced the Academy Award-winning film *Ordinary People* and the Oscar-nominated *A Soldier's Story*. A frequent collaborator with producer, director, and actor Sydney Pollack, his credits include *Tootsie, Meet Joe Black, Sabrina, Scent of a Woman,* and *Random Hearts.*

Tom Shadyac

At the age of twenty-three, Tom Shadyac became the youngest staff writer ever to pen jokes for comedian Bob Hope. He went on to direct, write, and produce some of America's best-loved comedies. He directed the Jim Carrey hits *Ace Ventura: Pet Detective; Liar, Liar,* and *Bruce Almighty,* which won the People's Choice Award for Best Comedy. He also directed *The Nutty Professor* with Eddie Murphy and directed and produced *Dragonfly* and *Patch Adams.*

Shadyac

Tony Shalhoub

The actor Tony Shalhoub charmed audiences with his four-time Emmy Award-winning role in *Monk,* a USA Network television series about an obsessive-compulsive detective. He also won a Tony, a Golden Globe Award, and a Screen Actor's Guild Award nomination. After earning a Master's degree from Yale Drama School, he worked on Broadway, where he received a Tony Award nomination for *Conversations with My Father.* In addition to *Monk,* he has appeared in the sitcoms *Wings* and *Stark Raving Mad.* His film credits include *Men in Black, Spy Kids, Thirteen Ghosts, The Siege, A Life Less Ordinary, Gattaca, Barton Fink,* and *Big Night,* for which the National Society of Film Critics honored him with the award for Best Supporting Actor.

Shalhoub

Vic Tayback

Vic Tayback appeared in numerous films and television shows during his lifetime, but you probably know him best as Mel from the TV sitcom *Alice.* He has acted in films such as *Treasure Island, The Choir Boys, Papillon,* and *The Gambler.* His television credits span five decades and include *Murder She Wrote, Bewitched, F-Troop, Daniel Boone,* and *Mission Impossible.* He was also the voice of Carface in the animated hit *All Dogs Go to Heaven.*

Did You Know? In 1970, Paul Orfalea started a major national retail chain, which he named after his curly hair. For this and other achievements, he was named 1997 Entrepreneur of the Year by the University of Southern California's Business School. What business did Orfalea start? *(answer on following page)*

179

Danny Thomas

Danny Thomas

Star of Emmy Award-winning sitcoms *The Danny Thomas Hour* and *Make Room for Daddy*, Danny Thomas was one of the most popular entertainers of the 1950s, 1960s, and 1970s. Beginning his career as a singer in nightclubs, he went on to perform for five U.S. presidents, from Franklin D. Roosevelt to Lyndon Baines Johnson. He was also a producer and worked with Sheldon Leonard on television comedies such as the *Andy Griffith Show* and the *Dick Van Dyke Show*. In 1962, he realized his dream of opening a hospital in honor of the saint whom he felt had helped him in his career. Today, St. Jude Children's Research Hospital in Memphis, Tennessee is one of the world's premier centers for researching and treating catastrophic diseases in children.

Marlo Thomas

Marlo Thomas, playing a modern single woman, starred in the TV show *That Girl*, which premiered in 1966. Some consider her to be primetime's first feminist! She won a Golden Globe, then co-produced, performed in, and won an Emmy for *Free to Be...You and Me*. The daughter of entertainer Danny Thomas, she won an Emmy in 1986 for *Nobody's Child* and another for hosting the *Body Human: Facts for Girls*. Her guest appearance on Friends won her an Emmy nomination.

Tony Thomas

Tony Thomas produced both the Emmy Award-winning *Brian's Song* and *Dead Poet's Society*, which was nominated for Best Picture at the Academy Awards. The son of the entertainer Danny Thomas, he produced the sitcoms *Soap, Benson, Empty Nest,* and *Blossom*, as well as the Emmy winner *Golden Girls*.

Tony and Marlo Thomas

Answer: Kinko's.

Tiffany

This 1980's pop idol was the first teenage singer to have her first two singles hit No. 1 on the Billboard music charts. Best known for the songs "I Think We're Alone Now," "Could've Been," and "I Saw Him Standing There," she also provided the voice of Judy Jetson in the 1990 movie *The Jetsons*.

Amy Yasbeck

Amy Yasbeck has appeared in everything from soap operas to hit movies. Her work on television includes roles in *Days of Our Lives, Wings, House Blend,* and *Dead Husbands*. On the big screen, she has appeared in *Pretty Woman, Problem Child, The Mask, Robin Hood: Men in Tights*, and *Home for the Holidays*. She started her career as a little girl, when her picture was featured on the box for Betty Crocker's Easy Bake Oven.

David Yazbek

If you like *Late Night with David Letterman* or the Broadway musical *The Fully Monty*, then you've enjoyed the work of David Yazbek. He won a Drama Desk Award for penning *The Full Monty*'s music and lyrics. He also won an Emmy for his work as a writer for David Letterman. In 1991, he collaborated on the theme song for the PBS children's show *Where in the World Is Carmen Santiago?* He went on to record two children's albums.

Tiffany

Photo Credits

Bilal Mcdad
Coming to America 20–21, 23, 24, 37, 46, 49, 50, 56, 58, 63, 64. *Living in America* 74–75, 76, 77, 78, 81, 84, 85, 86, 88, 89, 92, 94, 98, 104, 110, 112, 116, 117, 118, 124, 125, 127, 128, 129, 130, 131, 132, 135, 136. *Making an Impact* 138–39, 140, 148, 156, 160, 163, 170

Devon Akmon
Coming to America 31 (bell), 34, 47 (coin, key and pad), 51, 57, 58 (dress), 59, 60, 62, 67, 69. *Living in America* 87, 92 (button and patch), 93, 97, 103, 105, 106, 107, 112 (Hamady bag), 119, 121, 127 (detail of instruments). *Making an Impact* 159 (Maloof chair), 162 (Said's glasses), 164, 174 (Paul Anka's Sheet of Music), 175, 176

Laszlo Regos
8, 10, 182–83, 192

Index